T0345952

MODERN STUDY OF THE OLD TESTAMENT

AND

INSPIRATION

MODERN STUDY OF THE OLD TESTAMENT

AND

INSPIRATION

BY

T. H. SPROTT, M.A.

VICAR OF ST PAUL'S, WELLINGTON, N. Z.

"When interpreted like any other book, by the same rules of evidence
and the same canons of criticism, the Bible will still remain unlike
any other book."—JOWETT.

"Truth is the healer of its own wounds."—CHEYNE.

Cambridge :
at the University Press
1909

CAMBRIDGE UNIVERSITY PRESS
Cambridge, New York, Melbourne, Madrid, Cape Town,
Singapore, São Paulo, Delhi, Tokyo, Mexico City

Cambridge University Press
The Edinburgh Building, Cambridge CB2 8RU, UK

Published in the United States of America by
Cambridge University Press, New York

www.cambridge.org
Information on this title: www.cambridge.org/9781107600539

First published 1909
First paperback edition 2011

A catalogue record for this publication is available from the British Library

ISBN 978-1-107-60053-9 Paperback

TO

E. C. S.

PREFATORY NOTE

THIS book contains the substance, with considerable expansion, of lectures delivered in Lent 1902. It is published in deference to the wishes of some friends, who have also most generously made themselves responsible for the cost of publication. To these friends I wish to express my sincerest gratitude. Whatever may be its public fate, the book will always be to me the symbol of a great and undeserved goodwill. Nevertheless it was with much reluctance that I consented to publish it. I have always felt that no one is entitled to write a book who has not some contribution, at once original and valuable, to make to the subject dealt with. And this book can lay no claim to originality. I have but put together the results of such study as I have been able to give to books dealing with the problems of the Old Testament. In the appended list of authors and in footnotes I have indicated the sources to which I am chiefly indebted for thought and suggestion, and not seldom even for forms of phraseology. Doubtless my unconscious obligations extend still more widely. This much, however, I may claim, that I have not put down anything that has not seemed to me probable and reasonable. A certain negative element will be found in the book; but I trust that, if the positive and constructive element did not greatly preponderate, no persuasions of friends could have induced me to publish it. Man cannot live by negations alone; and he does his fellows but ill service who is content merely to be a critic of old beliefs. In the inevitable hours of "mortal moral strife" what is positive can alone sustain us.

I have gratefully to acknowledge the kindness of Mr Thos. Campbell, of the firm of Messrs Martin & Atkinson, in type-writing the entire book. I have also to thank Mr Stuart Sprott for kind assistance in reading the proof sheets, and Dr Barnes, Hulsean Professor of Divinity at Cambridge, for seeing this work through the Press.

T. H. S.

WELLINGTON, N. Z.,
March, 1909.

LIST OF BOOKS

Barnes, W. E., *Isaiah* (2 vols.), The Churchman's Bible.

Barrett, *The Bible and its Inspiration*.

Briggs, C. A., *International Critical Commentary on the Psalms*.

Bruce, A. B., *The Providential Order. Apologetics. The Chief End of Revelation*.

Budde, K., *Religion of Israel to the Exile*.

Charles, R. H., *Eschatology*.

Cheyne, T. K., *Origin of the Psalter*.

Cook, S. A., *The Laws of Moses and the Code of Hammurabi*.

Davidson, A. B., *Theology of the Old Testament*.

Driver, S. R., *Introduction to the Old Testament. Commentary on Genesis. Isaiah: his Life and Times*.

Gray, G. Buchanan, *The Divine Discipline of Israel*.

Haupt, P., *The Polychrome Bible*.

King, L. W., *The Seven Tablets of Creation*.

Kirkpatrick, A. F., *The Divine Library. The Doctrine of the Prophets*.

McFadyen, J. E., *Old Testament Criticism and the Christian Church. Messages of the Psalms*.

Maurice, J. F. D., *Patriarchs and Lawgivers. Prophets and Kings*.

Nash, *History of the Higher Criticism*.

Pinches, *The Old Testament in the Light of the Historical Records of Assyria and Babylonia*.

Peters, *Early Hebrew Story.*

Ryle, H. E. [Bp], *The Early Narratives of Genesis. The Canon of the Old Testament.*

Sanday, W., *Bampton Lectures. The Oracles of God.*

Sayce, *Genesis*, The Temple Bible.

Simon, D. W., *The Bible Theocratic Literature.*

Smith, G. A., *Modern Criticism and the Preaching of the Old Testament.*

Smith, H. P., *Old Testament History.*

Smith, W. R., *The Prophets of Israel. The Old Testament in the Jewish Church. The Religion of the Semites.*

Stanley, *History of the Jewish Church.*

Wellhausen, *History of Israel.*

Zenos, *The Elements of the Higher Criticism.*

CONTENTS

CHAPTER I

MODERN CRITICISM

IT is always difficult, perhaps impossible, accurately to fix the precise moment at which any great intellectual movement begins. Human thought is continuous not spasmodic, and movements which seem to begin to-day, may have their sources far back in the past. Bearing this fact in mind, we may, perhaps, say that the beginnings of modern Biblical Criticism are to be found in three names :—(1) Richard Simon, a Roman Catholic scholar, who in 1680 pointed out the existence of duplicate accounts of the same events in the Book of Genesis, and suggested as the explanation that Moses in writing the Book had used different authors; (2) Astruc, a French Roman Catholic physician, who in 1753 published a work, *Conjectures on the Original Memoirs of which it appears Moses made use in composing the Book of Genesis*, in which he pointed out that the duplicate accounts, e.g., of the Creation, were marked by the use of different terms for God, one speaking of the Creator as ELOHIM, the other as JEHOVAH or JEHOVAH-ELOHIM ; (3) Semler, a Protestant scholar (born 1725), who applied to the Bible the principles of historical study which he had learnt in the study of the "Humanities"—history and the classics[1].

The movement, then, is not of yesterday; it has been proceeding for something like two hundred years. For a time the methods used, and the results obtained, were confined to the learned few; but now through the medium of popular hand-books, reviews, magazines, and even newspapers, they have become, or are rapidly becoming, public property. Almost everybody now knows that a profound change of view, primarily in regard to the Old Testament, but also affecting the New Testament, has taken place in the minds of many scholars and thoughtful men. It cannot be denied that, in consequence, disquietude and anxiety are widespread, especially among good and devout people. Among these there is a more or less vague feeling that the movement has touched, or has seemed to touch, the very foundations of Christian faith; while lighter and more trifling minds have made the movement a reason, or perhaps it would be truer to say an excuse, for open and pronounced scepticism. In such circumstances it seems to me that every clergyman, pledged, as he was, at the most solemn moment of his life "to be diligent in reading of Holy Scriptures, and in such studies as help to a knowledge of the same", is bound to make himself acquainted, as

---

[1] Three other names, belonging to the sphere of general literature, must be mentioned as of epochal importance in the history of criticism—(1) Bentley, who by his *Dissertation on the Epistles of Phalaris* (1699) taught the learned that the authorship of ancient books cannot be at once determined by the traditional titles which they bear, but requires a careful examination of their contents. (2) Wolf, whose *Pro-legomena to Homer* (1795) showed that an ancient book, traditionally regarded as having a single author, may yet be of composite origin and of various age. (3) Niebuhr, who in his *History of Rome* (1811) showed the large part played by myth and legend in primitive history. See Beard's *Reformation of the Sixteenth Century*, pp. 202 ff. (abridged edition).

far as may be, with this critical movement, and that he is further bound to give to the people committed to his charge such help and guidance as he can. It is in an effort to fulfil this duty that I have undertaken the present course of lectures. I with the more confidence undertake the task, because already, by anticipation, in a course of lectures delivered last Lent (1901) I tried to show that the foundations of Christian faith are, to a large extent, independent of the results of criticism. Those of you who heard those lectures on "Some Grounds of Christian Certainty", may remember that I expressly abstained from using any theory as to the Divine inspiration or infallibility of the Bible; that I did not make, and did not need to make, any assumption regarding the Biblical writers other than that they were honest, painstaking, truthful men. The positive results of those lectures should be borne in mind, if in the present course I should seem to say anything negative or destructive of traditional belief.

Let me now point out the limits within which I think myself competent to deal with Biblical Criticism. I am not in any sense an expert; indeed to make this disclaimer may seem ridiculously superfluous. I am not entitled to express an authoritative opinion as to the extent to which many of the conclusions reached by critics have been fully established. He who would pronounce an authoritative opinion upon the whole field covered by criticism, must be an expert in at least the following subjects :—the Hebrew and cognate languages, the Greek language, the discoveries which have been made through the unearthing of the buried monuments of ancient Egyptian civilization and through the disinterring of the libraries of brick tablets which served for books in ancient Assyria and Babylonia; he must also be versed in historical method. It might be well for us to bear in mind this modest equipment of an expert in Biblical Criticism, and also to remember that, in all probability, it is not possessed by every writer of a pamphlet or magazine article or anonymous letter in the newspapers. The men possessing this equipment in any country of the world may, I suppose, be counted upon the fingers; in a country such as ours probably there is not one.

What, then, am I entitled to do? I am entitled to do neither more nor less than any fairly intelligent person is entitled to do, viz., to make myself familiar with the conclusions of Biblical Criticism, and to ask myself this question, What modifications, if any, supposing these conclusions to be proved, must I make in my inherited belief regarding the Bible, and consequently in my religious faith? (This statement as to what we non-experts are entitled to do, is made with respect to the conclusions of Biblical Criticism as a whole. There are, as we shall see, some of these conclusions which, with a Bible in our hands, we are quite competent to work out for ourselves.) This then is what an intelligent person is entitled to do, and, I think, is bound to do. The only advantage which I can have over any of you is that, having pledged myself to be diligent in such studies as help to a knowledge of the Holy Scriptures, I may perhaps possess—I certainly ought to possess—a somewhat fuller acquaintance with the subject than you who have placed yourselves under no such vow.

Let us now see what we mean by Modern Biblical Criticism. Of course the Bible has always been subject to criticism. Questions of authorship, text, structure, aim, must always have attracted intelligent students of the Bible. The Jewish Fathers who formed the Old Testament Canon must have used some kind of criticism when deciding what books were worthy, and what were not worthy, to be included in the Canon. Similarly, the early Christian Church, which out of the mass of early Christian writings selected the books which form the New Testament Canon, must have subjected those writings to some critical process, explicit or implicit. But in modern times the criticism of the Bible has come into a prominence, and been prosecuted with a thoroughness, unknown to any previous time. There are several reasons why this should be so.

First, we may assign a reason special to the circumstances of the Reformation Age. There were two causes in that age which led to a special prominence being given to the Bible. There was the Romanist taunt that, having rejected the authority of the infallible Church, Protestants must be without any sure guide in faith and morals. This taunt would not indeed have greatly troubled the first Reformers. The first Reformers were spiritual giants, and were sure that they had the promised presence of the Holy Spirit of God to guide them into all needful truth. But with the second generation it was different. The great enthusiasm was dying down. They were smaller men, and this Romanist taunt troubled them. Next, there was the rise within Protestantism of sectarian enthusiasts, who, by claiming special inner direct illumination from God, were producing an extreme individualism in religion, all too likely to end in complete disintegration and anarchy. Both Romanism and sectarianism were met by the exaltation of the Bible into a position of sole supremacy[1]. But Protestantism did not stop at this point. Panic-stricken it did not believe itself safe till it had made the most stupendous claims for the Bible—claims going far beyond anything that the Bible claimed for itself. It would not do to allow that it contained any human element whatever. Its writers were not simply the penmen of the Holy Spirit, they were His pens. Every word, every syllable, every comma, was dictated by God. A single illustration will show how extravagant much of this was. Almost everybody now knows that when the Hebrew language was a living tongue, its alphabet possessed no symbols for vowel-sounds. The consonants alone were written in any ancient Hebrew book, and the reader supplied the vowel-sounds from his own knowledge of the language. This may seem to you an almost impossible feat. Few of us could make much headway in reading an English book in which all the vowels were left out. But the structure of the Hebrew language is such that to read unvowelled Hebrew is for a fairly competent scholar a comparatively easy task. It was only when Hebrew had ceased to be a living tongue, and the pronunciation was in danger of being lost, that a set of vowel-signs was invented. This invention was not perfected till about the seventh century of our era. Accordingly the very latest of Old Testament books had been written fully eight hundred years before the language had a complete vowel notation. But this fact was not known in the Reformation Age. It was only as the study of Hebrew revived in the sixteenth and seventeenth

[1] See Dr D. W. Simon, *The Bible Theocratic Literature*, p. 14; also, Prof. H. S. Nash, *The History of the Higher Criticism of the New Testament*, p. 91.

centuries, that what men had once known regarding the history of the language was gradually recovered. The honour of discovering the true account of the vowel system belongs to a French Professor, Louis Cappel, who proclaimed his discovery in 1624. His discovery was received with a storm of opposition ; and as late as 1675 it was expressly laid down in one of the formularies of the Swiss Reformed Church that not only the consonants but the vowels of the Hebrew text were Divinely inspired. Could anything be further from what we now know to be a fact[1] !

Such then were the claims made for the Bible under the influence of the taunts of Romanists and the rise of fanatical sectarianism. The most important result was that the whole question of the Bible and its inspiration was definitely raised. In the past men had been content to believe that the Bible was the Word of God, without formulating any elaborately reasoned, technically exact, statement of the sense in which it was so, or of the relation in which the human writer stood to the Divine Inspirer. Henceforward this problem pressed for solution.

But in addition to the theological cause special to the Reformation Age, there have been general causes at work in modern times to stimulate criticism. There is the immense mental activity so characteristic of the modern world—the passion for investigation, for the discovery of truth. " The century ", says John Fiske, " which has just closed, which some have called an age " of iron, has been also an age of ideas ; an age of seeking " and finding, the like of which has never been known " before. It is an epoch the grandeur of which dwarfs

[1] See Dr W. Sanday, *The Oracles of God*, p. 20.

" all others that can be named since the beginning of the
" historic period, if not since man first became dis-
" tinctively human.   In their mental habits, in their
" methods of enquiry, and in the data at their command,
" the men of the present day who have kept pace with
" the scientific movement are separated from the men
" whose education ended in 1830 by an immeasurably
" wider gulf than ever before divided one progressive
" generation of men from their predecessors."   Nothing
has escaped this passion for investigation.   All the
extant literatures of the world have been swept into the
current.   There were special reasons why the Bible
should not escape.   The modern sciences of Astronomy,
Geology, Anthropology, the discoveries in Babylonia and
Assyria, the science of Comparative Religion, seemed
sharply to clash with statements contained in the Bible,
or with doctrines deduced from it.   Such, roughly, have
been the causes of Modern Biblical Criticism.   It differs
from all ancient criticism chiefly in two respects:—
(1) Its method is more exact and scientific.   Ancient
Biblical Criticism, so far as there was such a thing, shared
the defects of all ancient science.   It was carried on
somewhat at random, and the true principles of scientific
investigation had not been thoroughly thought out and
formulated.   In modern days these principles have been
thought out and formulated.   That they are the true
principles of investigation has been proved by their
amazing success.   As Dr Russel Wallace points out, the
discoveries made by modern method exceed those of all
preceding time.   Modern Biblical Criticism has been
able to avail itself of these exacter and more scientific
methods.   (2) It differs also in the immensely greater
accumulation of data which it has at command—e.g., all

the materials comprised under the heads of Egyptology and Assyriology.

At what, then, does Modern Criticism aim? There are, as probably you know, two great departments of criticism, usually called " Lower Criticism " and " Higher Criticism". These terms are exceedingly unsatisfactory. The qualifying words " Lower " and " Higher " do not, as all such qualifying terms should do, clearly distinguish the one Criticism from the other, or indicate what is the subject-matter of either critical method. You might think that they were meant to distinguish them as elementary and advanced respectively; but that view would be a mistake. The terms were invented by Eichhorn, a German scholar, belonging to the latter half of the eighteenth and the first quarter of the nineteenth centuries. Succeeding scholars have attempted to find more intelligible terms, but without success. What the terms are intended to mean I shall now try to explain[1].

There are several questions which may be asked regarding every book which comes into our hands, though some of these questions apply more particularly to ancient books. We may ask, Have we the text of the book exactly as the author wrote it? Are we sure that no alterations, more or less serious, have accidentally got into it, either through printers' errors, if it be a modern book, or copyists' errors, if it be an ancient book? Are we sure that no deliberate alteration has been made by some one other than the original author? Are we sure that there have been no omissions or additions? We know that the texts of books are liable to be altered in these ways. Accidental errors have of course been

[1] In what follows I am largely indebted to Professor A. C. Zenos's admirable book, *The Elements of the Higher Criticism.*

reduced to a minimum by modern methods of printing, though, even so, they do occur, and few modern books are absolutely free from such mistakes. So too our modern sense of an author's property in his book—a sense not keen amongst the ancients—prevents deliberate alteration of what he has written, except in the case of hymns, which the compilers of our hymn-books seem to think they may alter at will. Thus, the hymn "Lead kindly Light" has been altered by addition in at least one hymn-book; and "When I survey the wondrous Cross" has likewise been altered by addition, to the detriment of its theology, in our own hymn-book; and there are many other instances. But in the case of ancient books, copied by many hands, and in ages when there was no strong sense of an author's property in what he had written, such alterations, accidental and deliberate, were much more frequent. Now we wish to know whether the text of the Bible has suffered in these ways; and, if so, to what extent. We wish to know whether the text, as we have it, is pure; and if not, whether we have any means of correcting the errors that have crept into it. This is the work of the Lower Criticism.

The method by which the Lower Criticism seeks to solve its problem is much too elaborate and complicated to be set forth in such a lecture as the present. It is enough to say that it proceeds by comparing all available copies of the book. If they all agreed verbally, there would be a strong presumption that we had the original text, for a multitude of copyists in different countries and ages would not be likely to make just the same mistakes. Even then there would not of course be absolute certainty, for all extant copies might ultimately have been made not from the author's autograph, but from some one subsequent copy into which corruptions had already entered. If the extant copies are found to differ, we should then have to decide, by a variety of considerations, which copies are most likely to have preserved the true text. Now to this lower criticism the Bible, or at least the New Testament, has been most searchingly subjected. As a result the MSS. of the New Testament have indeed been found to vary, but the variation is wonderfully limited and unimportant[1]. The results hitherto obtained are, roughly speaking, embodied in the Revised Version of the New Testament; for the Revised Version is not merely a revision of the English Version of 1611, but also of the Greek text upon which that version was based.

Not nearly so much progress has been made in the textual criticism of the Old Testament. It is known, indeed, that our extant Old Testament MSS. have not in all respects preserved the original text. We know this by comparing them with ancient translations—the Latin, the Syriac, the Aramaic paraphrases, known as the Targums, and, above all, the Greek, known as the Septuagint, which belongs to the third or second century B.C. Such comparison shows that the translators had before them a Hebrew text differing in some respects from the Hebrew text now extant, and also in some respects superior to it. The reasons why so little has been done for the text of the Old Testament as compared with the New Testament are briefly these. All our extant MSS. of the Old

[1] See Westcott and Hort, *New Testament in the Original Greek*, p. 565: "If comparative trivialities, "such as changes of order, the "insertion or omission of the article "with proper names, and the like, "are set aside, the words in our "opinion still subject to doubt can "hardly amount to more than a "thousandth part of the whole New "Testament".

Testament are pronounced by scholars to be manifestly
copies of one and the same early MS.   By examination
of these we can determine what was the text of that
parent MS.   But then the question arises, Is *it* a perfectly
accurate transcript of the autograph, or have any errors
crept in ?   To answer this question we are thrown back
upon the ancient translations already mentioned.   But
here two difficulties arise.   Those ancient translations
may themselves have suffered more or less of corruption
in the course of transmission, and may require critical
revision.   And, even then, it would not always be
possible to determine what Hebrew text the translators
must have had before them.   For these reasons hardly
any textual revision was attempted in the Revised
Version of the Old Testament.   In the case of the New
Testament, on the other hand, our extant MSS. which
are vastly more numerous than those of any other ancient
writing, group themselves into families descended from
independent copies of the apostolic writings.   Now inasmuch as independent copyists are in the highest degree
unlikely to make exactly the same slips, it becomes
morally certain that where the ancestors of our present
MSS. agree, we have an accurate transcript of the
original text.

A critical text of the Old Testament, embodying the
results of both lower and higher criticism, is being prepared by some forty European and American scholars.
But whether, when completed, if it ever be completed, it
will gain general acceptance among those competent to
judge, is a question upon which we can express no opinion.
But, meantime, for our reassurance this may be confidently said, that in the Old Testament, as in the New
Testament, the limits of textual error have been ascer-

tained, and it is certain that we have substantially what the authors wrote. The manuscripts of the Bible have not, indeed, been miraculously preserved through the ages, any more than the manuscripts of other ancient books, from the mistakes which all copyists and editors are liable to make. But they are *mistakes*. Of deliberate tampering with the text of the Bible for dogmatic purposes there is little or no trace. We have this treasure, like all other Divine treasures, in an earthern vessel. The vessel shows some of the cracks and flaws of age; but when one remembers what vicissitudes it has passed through, it is in marvellously good condition, and its Divine treasure is intact.

Such, then, roughly, is the work of the Lower Criticism. It deals with the question, Have we, at this late date, or can we hope to recover, what the Biblical authors actually wrote?

But there are other questions that we may ask regarding any book which may come into our hands.

Thus we may ask, By whom was the book written? Now the book itself may contain this information on its title page; but this does not necessarily settle the question. We know that such titles are sometimes forgeries; or the name may be, as in the case of many modern novels, an innocent pseudonym. Again, the book may be itself anonymous, but tradition or popular conjecture may have assigned a name to its author. Now we know that popular conjecture and tradition are sometimes mistaken. *In Memoriam* first appeared anonymously, and the most absurd guesses were made as to the author, e.g., that it was written by the widow of an army man! The Athanasian Creed was, as its very name shows, ascribed by tradition to Athanasius.

Later investigation has shown that it not only was not, but could not have been, written by him. It contains forms of speech which Athanasius would not have accepted. Or, again, a book may be absolutely anonymous neither bearing a name upon its title page, nor having one popularly ascribed to it.

Now, it is true that in the case of some books the question of authorship, and the cognate questions of date and place, may be unimportant. This is true, for example, of purely imaginative literature. The value of such literature lies in the truth and beauty of its ideas and form, and these we perceive for ourselves, or not at all. But in the case of other classes of literature these questions may be of very great importance indeed. If I am reading a medical work, it is well to know whether it is the work of a mere layman or quack, or of a trained, experienced, and competent physician. So, too, a knowledge of date and place may be of importance. The environment, physical and social[1], in which the author lived, the influences to which he was subjected, may have much to do with the value and meaning of his work.

But a further question may arise regarding authorship. A book may bear an author's name on the title page, yet this may hold good only of a portion of the contents; a part may be due to some one else whose name does not appear. This binding together within one cover of the writings of two or more authors may come about quite accidentally. For example, the late Boer war was prolific in pamphlets, etc. Some of these writings set forth the causes of the war; some gave accounts of various episodes in its course; some were

---

[1] Social environment includes the readers for whom the book was in-tended, and whose circumstances may have determined its contents.

written by military experts, others by civilians; some
by strong partisans, others by impartial observers; some
by eye-witnesses, others upon hearsay; some gave their
authors' names, others were anonymous, and others,
again, perhaps, pseudonymous. Now let us suppose
that you have a collection of these writings, and that
they are nearly all anonymous, or that in course of time
the title pages of most of them get torn off. In
order to preserve them you have them all bound in
one volume, placing first the pamphlet which bore an
author's name, either quite accidentally, or because it
dealt with the earliest stages of the war. Interest in
the war having died away, your miscellaneous volume
lies on some dusty shelf. But fifty years hence something happens to revive men's interest in the events of
1899–1902. There arises a demand for contemporary
literature. An enterprising Wellington publisher of
the day learns of the existence of your old book. He
purchases it; publishes an edition; and, as he finds only
one author's name, the book appears under the title
Contemporary Record of the Great Boer War, by ——.
Here, then, by a series of not very improbable accidents,
a number of writings, just because they deal with the
same subject-matter, get ascribed to one author, though,
in reality, the work of several, with some of whom the
reputed author would have violently disagreed. And of
what varying value the book would be! For, as we
have seen, military experts and civilians, partisans and
non-partisans, those who were eye-witnesses and those
who were not, all shared in its production. What a
problem your innocent little collection of pamphlets
would present to the literary student!

You see, then, how, even in modern times, a book

may come to have a composite authorship, while yet it bears the name of only one writer. There is a special reason why this might happen—did in fact happen—in the case of ancient books. Ancient books, as we know, were not printed by machinery, but copied by hand. Often you would make your own copy. Now the parchment used was exceedingly costly, and it would be your desire not to waste any portion of it. Accordingly, if, when you had copied one work, you had still some space remaining, nothing was more natural than to copy something else on it. Now let us suppose that the first work you copied had the author's name, and that the second was anonymous, nothing would be more natural than that, in course of time, both writings should come to be ascribed to the same author. There are phenomena in the Bible of which this *may be* the explanation. For example, critics believe that our present Book of Isaiah is of composite origin, and that the last twenty-seven chapters were not written by Isaiah. It would be impossible here to set forth all the grounds of this conclusion, but the most easily understood are the following. The last twenty-seven chapters deal, for the most part, with the Return from Captivity in 536 B.C. They *seem* to have been written on the eve of the Return. Cyrus, who granted the Return, is brought before us in the midst of his career of conquest. Now Isaiah lived and worked in the second half of the eighth century (740–700 B.C.), more than a hundred and fifty years before the Return; and it is with his own times that the preceding part of the book deals. Now it is, of course, conceivable that Isaiah was inspired by God to write about what should happen some century and a half after his death. But when we add that the style and religious ideas of the later chapters differ from those of the earlier chapters, the probabilities seem to point to a distinct author contemporary with the eve of the Return. Now if this later writer[1] published his work anonymously, wishing for some reason to be regarded, to use his own words, merely as "a voice"; and if some early copyist, wishing to economise his material, copied the work on a roll which already contained the writings of Isaiah, we can understand how later uncritical ages might come to imagine Isaiah to be the author of the whole. Another example of confusion of authorship, which is, possibly, to be explained in the same way, is to be found in the well-known difficulty in St Matthew xxvii. 9. The Evangelist in illustration of the purchase of the potter's field with the blood-money which Judas could not keep, quotes a passage from ancient prophecy, " Then was fulfilled that which was spoken by Jeremiah the Prophet", etc. When we turn to the Old Testament we find that the passage in question was spoken not by Jeremiah, but by Zechariah. This may of course be due to a mere slip of memory on the part of the Evangelist; but it may just as well be due to the fact that the Books of Jeremiah and Zechariah were written on the same roll, if not universally, at least in the circles with which one Evangelist was associated, and spoken of together as the " Prophet Jeremiah ".

An exceedingly curious illustration of the scarcity and costliness of parchment or vellum in ancient days is afforded by what are known as Palimpsest MSS., that is, MSS. from which the original writing has been erased

---

[1] I am of course aware that many critics believe that more than one writer had a hand in the composition of the later chapters. The point does not materially affect the argument.

or washed off in order that they might be utilized for
fresh matter in which the living generation took more
interest.   This process of erasure, however, was seldom
so fully carried out but that the earlier writing might
still be traced more or less completely under the more
modern writing.   Some of our most precious MSS. are
of this description.   For example, in the library of my
own University there is a MS. of St Matthew's Gospel
belonging to the fifth century.   In the tenth century
some one washed off St Matthew's text and used the
vellum for copying a treatise of St Chrysostom on the
Priesthood, but St Matthew's text can still be discerned
beneath St Chrysostom's.   In the British Museum there
is an exceedingly curious example, in which the washing
off process has been done twice over.   The vellum was
first used for a copy of St John's Gospel, over which was
written a Syriac work, which, in its turn, was washed off
and the vellum used for a second Syriac work.   All
three writings are still discernible[1].   It may seem to
you strange that anyone should erase the words of the
Bible in order to use the parchment for other writings,
sometimes of little value.   But the whole thing illustrates
the scarcity and costliness of writing material.

But to return; there is another point in this matter
of authorship to which I must call your attention.   Books
may be pseudonymous : the names which the books bear
may not be the names of the real authors.   This, as we
have seen, may be due to accident.   The book may have
been published anonymously, and the reading public
may have thought they detected the author, naming
some well-known man, whose name comes in course

---

[1] Scrivener, *Introduction to the Criticism of the New Testament*, Vol. I.
p. 141.

of time to be attached to the book. But the author himself may have chosen to write under an assumed name. Many of our modern novelists adopt this practice. So long as the name chosen is not that of some real personage whose name would win for the book a vogue which it did not intrinsically merit, there is nothing immoral in this proceeding. Or, the name used may be that of a real personage, but of one long since dead whose name has become typical of the subject of which the writer is treating. Here, again, if there is no attempt at imitation of style, no attempt to put forth the book as a long-lost treasure discovered ; if the writer speaks as a man of his own time and place, there is no violation of morality. For example, the noblest of the Apocryphal Books is put forth under the name of Solomon, *The Wisdom of Solomon.* Now the author was not King Solomon, but an Alexandrian Jew of the first century B.C. Nevertheless the book is not a forgery, for it bears no sign of any attempt to palm it off as a veritable work of the wise king. Solomon's name had become a synonym for wisdom, and it was a perfectly natural thing for one who wished to put forth reflections upon life and conduct to use the personality of the typically wise man as his literary vehicle.

Such then are some of the questions which may be asked concerning the authorship of any book.

Another question which may be asked is, What is the literary form of the book ? Is it poetry or is it prose ? This is, of course, a question which, except in sarcasm, we should not ask about a modern book. Modern books are so described in their very titles and so printed that it is impossible to mistake to what class

of literature they belong.   One need not enter upon
an elaborate investigation to discover that Tennyson's
In Memoriam is a poem ; he is told that it is such on
the title page; he sees that it is such by the arrangement
of the text in lines, verses, and stanzas.   An ancient
reader had not these aids.   "Poetry and prose alike were
written in consecutive manuscript".   The Authorised
Version of the Bible, in which the poetical parts of the
Old Testament are printed just like the prose parts,
is in this respect faithful to ancient method.   In the
Revised Version our modern method of distinguishing
poetry from prose for the eye is adopted.   The ancient
practice occasioned no difficulty to ancient men who
were familiar with it.   But it is a real and serious
difficulty for us who are not familiar with it, especially
in dealing with Hebrew poetry, which differs from prose,
not, as does our own poetry, by metre[1] and rhyme, but
by elevation of diction and parallelism of thought.   Yet,
properly to distinguish literary forms is a matter of
the highest importance.   You certainly need to know
whether what you are reading is meant to be taken
as simple matter of fact, or is a work of emotion and
imagination.   Not a few of the absurdities and crudities
of popular religion are due to nothing but a confusion
of Biblical poetry with prose.   The Revised Version
has done much to indicate typographically the poetic
elements of the Old Testament, but it has left much yet
to be done.   We have, for example, in the second chapter
of Genesis a snatch of poetry which the Revised Version

---

[1] I am aware that many modern
scholars hold that Hebrew poetry
is metrical ; but there seems to be
little agreement as to the laws of
metre.

has failed to print as such. It is Adam's exclamation of surprised joy when Eve is presented to him—

> "This is now bone of my bone,
>   And flesh of my flesh:
> Woman shall she be called,
>   For from man was she taken".

Yet another question that may be asked regarding any book is, What is its value? The value of a book depends upon the extent to which it fulfils the purpose or purposes for which books of the class to which it belongs are written. If, for example, the book belongs to the class of history, then its value will depend upon the trustworthiness of its information regarding, and its success in discovering the principles at work in, the period with which it deals. It is important to notice that a book may have several values, and may be more valuable in some respects than in others. In other words, the writer may have more than one end in view, and he may be more successful in achieving some one of these ends than the others. A novelist, for example, may mean his story to be not merely a work of fiction pure and simple to amuse and entertain, but also to be the vehicle of historical information, or of a moral and religious lesson. Now his book may have value in some of these respects, while it is valueless in others. As a story it may be highly entertaining, while its history is untrustworthy, and its moral and religious teaching poor or erroneous; or, as a story it may be poor, while its history may be informing, and its moral and religious teaching lofty and inspiring. Now in judging the value of the book it is important to discover which of these ends was paramount with the author. If, for example, his chief aim was historical, then, if his history is untrustworthy, his book is of little value, no matter how entertaining its story or inspiring its moral teaching; and so on.

Such then are the main questions which we may ask regarding any book that may come into our hands. We may ask, Have we the genuine text? Do we know the author, his date and place? Is it Poetry or Prose, History or Romance, Philosophy or Science? Does it fulfil the purpose for which all books of its class are written? To answer these questions is the task of criticism. The criticism which deals with the text is called "Lower Criticism"; that which deals with authorship, etc. is called "Higher Criticism". As I have already remarked, these terms "Lower" and "Higher" are unfortunate; the latter especially so, as it has suggested to some minds an offensive claim to superior knowledge. In reality no such claim is made or implied. The term "Higher" is relative to "Lower", and is meant to suggest that the Criticism which it designates is a superstructure of which that designated "Lower" is the foundation. Obviously, we must be sure of our text before we can profitably discuss questions of authorship, etc.

Such then being what we mean by Criticism it is plain that criticism is not confined to the Bible; it deals with all books whatsoever; it is implied in the intelligent use of any and every book. True, we do not set ourselves to ask and answer these questions as to text, authorship, etc. every time a new book comes into our hands; but that is simply because in the vast majority of modern books we already know, or think we know, the answers. Modern methods of printing are so accurate that we assume the text is correct, or, if not, a table of errata will be supplied in the book itself; while the modern sense of an author's rights is so keen that we are sure there has been no deliberate tampering. The title page will give, though of course not always, the author's name, date, place. The typographical arrangement will show whether the book is poetry or prose. The value of the book is guaranteed by the author's name, or by criticisms in reviews; and so on. But in cases where we do not know the answers, then, if we are intelligent users of books, we at once become critics, "Lower" and "Higher". And if we ourselves do not know the methods by which our questions can be answered, or are unskilled in the use of them, we turn to those whom we know to be experts, and accept, provisionally at least, their conclusions.

Criticism, I say, in both its departments, is implied in all intelligent use of books. How absurd then it is to condemn criticism *per se.* It is legitimate to try to show that the conclusions which critics have reached are not the conclusions to which the right use of critical methods leads. If critics, or any of them, display an irreverent spirit, it is right to condemn that spirit. But to condemn Criticism itself is simply to proscribe the exercise of intelligence in our study of the Bible.

CHAPTER II

RESULTS OF CRITICISM

In the preceding lecture I tried to give you a rough account of what is meant by Criticism, its methods and aims. We saw that there were two Criticisms to which all books may be subjected, usually designated "Lower" and "Higher". For completeness' sake, I gave you some account of the former; but for the remainder of these lectures our concern will be exclusively with the latter. I have now to give you some account of the results which higher critics claim to have reached. In this account I shall confine myself to such results as have been accepted by critical scholars generally; with the speculations of individual scholars we have no concern. This is only what we do in all other subjects requiring expert knowledge, as, for example, the various sciences. On the one hand, the mere layman, on pain of being convicted of arrogance, must accept, at least provisionally, the conclusions about which the great body of experts in the given subject are agreed. On the other hand, were he at once to accept the hypotheses of some one or two experts, as against the general concensus of expert opinion, he would be no less guilty of intellectual frivolity. Such intellectual frivolity is not unknown in the sphere of Biblical Criticism. I have heard of laymen who have accepted as proved a Dutch scholar's theory that none of the Pauline Epistles are genuine, though the said theory is scouted by the vast majority of experts, both in Europe and America. This I count pitiable frivolity. I have said we laymen must accept, *at least provisionally*, the general concensus of expert opinion. The qualification is necessary; for we must remember that *fashion* may reign in the sphere of Criticism as in other departments of human life, and that fashions have an element of unreason in them, and may easily change. In his posthumous work on *The Human Element in the Gospels* the late Dr Salmon points out how, in his early days, it was the fashion in critical circles to regard it as a sign of ignorance or immodesty not to accept the second century date then assigned by advanced critics to the New Testament writings. Well, how foolish anyone, who had unreservedly followed the critical fashion of that day, would look in these days, when the first century date of almost all these writings has been firmly re-established! There may be critical fashions to-day; and these fashions may change. We know how to-day, in the sphere of the Natural Sciences, conclusions, which, not long ago, were regarded as firmly established, are being revised in the light of fuller knowledge. The same thing may happen in the sphere of Old Testament Criticism. Accordingly, the wise man only provisionally accepts what is offered to him. It is the honest work of the scholarship of to-day; so he accepts it. It may, in some respects, be modified by the larger scholarship of to-morrow; so he puts in a saving clause. If it seem to you that the logical outcome of all this is a general scepticism, my reply is, that it is the aim of these lectures to show you that there is an element in the Bible that is independent of these mutations of human opinion.

What then are the results of the Higher Criticism that are generally accepted to-day?

I. We shall take first the questions of authorship and date. Well; for one thing, Criticism extends the area of anonymity. It was, of course, always recognised that there were anonymous writings in the Old Testament. No tradition, so far as I am aware, earlier than the Talmudic[1] names any authors for the Books of Judges, Ruth, Samuel, Kings, Chronicles, Job, Esther. These books derive their titles not from their authors, but, with more or less of accuracy, from their subject-matter. I may just remark that the very fact that there are admittedly anonymous books in the Old Testament, shows that a knowledge of authorship cannot be a matter of life and death. But by modern Criticism other books, or portions of books, are brought within the same category.

1. The Pentateuch, *as we have it*, is asserted to be the work, not of Moses in the thirteenth century B.C., but of an author or authors, unknown, in the fifth century B.C. Omitting Deuteronomy, the Pentateuch—or rather the Hexateuch[2], for Joshua is by modern scholars associated with the first five books—is the product of a combination of three main documents of varying antiquity. These documents have had names given to them, according to their way of designating the Divine Being in the pre-Mosaic period, and according to the prominence given to everything connected with law and worship. Thus,

---

[1] Baba Bathra 14b.
[2] Pentateuch = Five rolls : Hexateuch = Six rolls.

one document uses the name JEHOVAH (YAHAWEH or JAHVEH) for God in the pre-Mosaic period. It is, accordingly, called the Jehovistic Document, and is symbolised by J. J is supposed to have originated in the Southern Kingdom in the ninth century B.C. (later than Solomon), and to mark the beginning of Hebrew literature in the proper sense of the term. Doubtless before this period traditions, war-ballads and other songs were current; but they were chiefly passed about by word of mouth, or, even if some had been committed to writing, they had not been reduced to a true literary shape[1].

Another document uses ELOHIM as its name for God in the pre-Mosaic period, its view being that the name JEHOVAH was first communicated to Moses, and was previously unknown by the Hebrews. Accordingly it is called the Elohist Document, and is supposed to have originated in the eighth century B.C., and in the Northern Kingdom. It covers pretty much the same ground as J, except that it does not seem to have carried up the story beyond Abraham, whereas J goes back to the Creation. With the overthrow of the Northern Kingdom by the Assyrians in 721 B.C. the literature of the North passed, during the reign of Hezekiah, to the Judaean Kingdom, where the two documents, J and E, were combined into one history, styled by critics JE.

The third document is chiefly interested in all things pertaining to law and worship, and is accordingly called the Priestly Code, and is symbolised by P. To P belong Leviticus and the corresponding portions of the other books. Like J, P carries the history back to the Creation,

---

[1] See Peters, *Early Hebrew Story*, p. 4.

and to it we owe the noble "Psalm of Creation" in Gen. i.—ii. 4.   P is ascribed to the fifth century B.C.

Deuteronomy stands by itself. It first appears in history in the year 621 B.C., when it gave rise to Josiah's great reformation (2 Kings xxii.). It is supposed to have been written in the preceding reign of Manasseh. It may be said to be the first book of the Bible to receive canonical recognition. Towards the end of the fifth century P was combined with JE, and this combination, together with Deuteronomy, gives us our present Hexateuch, that is, the five Books of the Law with Joshua.

Such in very meagre outline is the modern theory of the origin of these first books of the Bible. It would be a grave mistake to regard it as a purely gratuitous theory. It is, with whatever success, a serious attempt to account for phenomena in these books that have puzzled all thoughtful readers. It has, indeed, been doubted whether it is possible thus to discriminate different documents in what is now one whole. Who, it has been asked, could with certainty single out the respective contributions of Besant and Rice in the joint work of those authors? But all such modern instances furnish no true parallel. Besant and Rice were contemporaries, living in the same social and intellectual environment; they deliberately collaborated; they did not each write a complete story, with the same plot and incidents, and then dovetail them into each other. On the other hand the authors of J, E, and P were separated from one another by centuries; P, for example, being separated from J by no less than four hundred years. Accordingly their whole environment, social, political, intellectual, religious, was different. They largely covered the same ground and dealt with the same incidents. And it is just because we find in the history, as it has come down to us, duplicate accounts of the same incidents, differing in vocabulary, point of view and theology, that the theory of plural authorship has been framed to account for the phenomenon.

As a further result of this investigation into the origin of the Pentateuch, the whole body of Pentateuchal legislation is no longer regarded as the direct work of Moses, promulgated by him in the Wilderness of Sinai and on the eve of the invasion of Canaan. The legal system of Israel is assimilated to the legal systems of other nations, which grow, develop, and undergo modifications, with the growing and changing national life. Three main legal codes, widely separated in time, are distinguished. (1) the Covenant Code, found in Ex. xx. 22—xxiii. 33 ; (2) the Deuteronomic Code ; (3) the Levitical Code. Of these Codes only the first, it is said, can be regarded as strictly Mosaic. The other two, separated from Moses by some six and eight centuries respectively, are Mosaic only in a secondary sense, as being legitimate developments of the original legislation.

So much, then, for the authorship and date of the Pentateuch. If it seem to you revolutionary, I would point out that the Pentateuch itself makes no claim to be the work of Moses. It does, indeed, speak of Moses as having written down certain things (Ex. xvii. 14, xxiv. 4, xxxiv. 27 ; Num. xxxiii. 2 ; Deut. xxxi. 9, 22, 24) ; but about its own authorship, as a whole, it is silent. The fact that specific things are mentioned as having been written by Moses, rather implies that he did not write the rest. It is to Jewish tradition we owe the theory of Mosaic authorship.

2. Though the Psalter has been traditionally called "The Psalms of David", yet tradition itself has always been aware that the title was not strictly accurate, many Psalms, as their headings show, having been by tradition ascribed to other authors. Nor, as regards Psalms to be ascribed to David, has tradition been uniform, the Septuagint following, in this respect, a tradition differing from that preserved in our present Hebrew text. The whole collection may have been called "Davidic" because David was regarded as the originator of Jewish Psalmody and its most illustrious exponent, and also, perhaps, its largest contributor. Here, too, Criticism has enlarged the area of anonymity. On the ground of internal evidence and the growth and development of religious ideas, David's connexion with the Psalter is reduced to the most meagre limits. Only a very few Psalms are assigned to David; some critics would allow him only one, the eighteenth; others, none at all. Much or most of the Psalter, and indeed by some critics the whole, is placed in the post-exilic age. But on the subject of the Psalter critical opinion is greatly divided, and there are scholars who maintain that the Psalter contains a tolerable number of pre-exilic psalms or fragments of psalms.

3. Substantially the same remark may be made regarding the Book of Proverbs. It is called, indeed, "The Proverbs of Solomon"; but that can only mean that Solomon was its most illustrious, and probably its earliest, contributor; for the Book itself tells us that it also contains wise sayings of other sages, for example, Agur (xxx.) and Lemuel (xxxi. 1–9). The specifically "Solomonic" portions are (1) chapters x. 1—xxii. 16 (which bear the title: "The Proverbs of Solomon");

(2) xxv.—xxix. (which bear the title: " These also are Proverbs of Solomon, which the men of Hezekiah copied out "). Chapters xxii. 17—xxiv. 34 are "words of the wise". It is probable that the Book is composed of minor collections, made at different times, and that it was edited in its present form about 300 B.C.

4. As we have already seen, the present Book of Isaiah is regarded as being in part anonymous, chapters i.—xxxix. being alone credited to Isaiah, the remainder being the work of an unknown author who lived on the eve of the Return (538 B.C.). It ought to be added that considerable portions of both sections are thought to be by other hands.

5. The Book of Zechariah is likewise thought to be in part anonymous, chapters i.—viii. being the work of Zechariah, the remainder, the work of two earlier and unknown Prophets.

6. Modern Criticism holds that at least two of the Old Testament Books are pseudonymous—viz. (*a*) Ecclesiastes, which purports to give the experiences of King Solomon in the tenth century, but is really a work of the third century; (*b*) Daniel, which, it is said, is not the work of Daniel in the Exile (586–536), but may quite confidently be assigned to the year 167 B.C., the time of the Maccabees.

Such, then, roughly are the results arrived at by modern Criticism in the matter of date and authorship. It cannot be denied that we experience some sense of loss, even though it be chiefly a sentimental loss. It is a loss to have cherished writings separated from great names in the past, and consigned to unknown authorship and a less venerable antiquity. At the end of this chapter I give a table of the dates of the Old Testament writings, as these are approximately determined by modern Criticism.

II.   We come now to what modern Criticism has to tell us of the literary forms of the Old Testament writings.   It has, of course, always been recognised that Biblical literature exhibits some of the literary forms with which our own and other literatures have made us familiar: Poetry, History, Oratory.

Modern Criticism enlarges the poetic element; and further assimilates Hebrew literature to other national literatures by adding the Drama (at least in undeveloped form as in Job and Canticles); the Idyll (Ruth); the Historic Romance (Esther); Myth and Legend (as in the early stories in Genesis and in portions of Judges). These last may be defined and contrasted as follows :— Myth is the spontaneous and unconscious creation by a people of a story out of an idea—thought expressed in the form of narrative.   It is, therefore, purely imaginative.   Legend is narrative having a basis in fact, springing up naturally among a people, and unconsciously amplified, abridged, modified, idealised, in accordance with popular feeling.   To put it briefly: Myth is historicised idea; Legend is idealised history.   As with other literatures, Myth and Legend belong to the pre-historic stage of Hebrew life.

III.   As to value; modern Criticism holds that the Biblical histories have not escaped the inaccuracies as to matter of fact which characterise all other historical writings.   Historians are dependent for their knowledge of past events upon tradition, and documentary and monumental evidence.   These are liable, in varying degree, to the errors that beset all human testimony, and in fact are often found to conflict.   A careful study of their writings show that the Hebrew historians had no other sources of information; nor were these sources, in their case, more free from occasional conflict in their testimony. This position of modern Criticism we can verify for ourselves. To take but a few examples; anyone who will carefully read and compare 1 Sam. viii.—xii.; xvi., xvii.; 2 Sam. xxiv., 1 Chron. xxi.; can see for himself that there are discrepancies in the accounts of the appointment of Saul as king; the first appearance of David at Saul's Court; David's census. The discrepancies are unimportant, but they exist. I have said that the sources of information upon which historians are dependent are, *in varying degree*, liable to error. It is important to notice the qualifying words "in varying degree", that we may not make the childish mistake of imagining that error is uniformly present in our history-books, and that, consequently, the whole narrative is vitiated. Let us see what were some of the sources which the Hebrew historians had at their command. (1) From the time of David and Solomon onwards the nation began to keep official records of its own life and doings. The Court had its Recorder or Official Chronicler. Biographies, too, of great men were written. All such documents, being contemporary or nearly contemporary, are first-class evidence and set us upon the ground of history. (2) For the ages preceding David and Solomon the historian was mainly dependent upon war-ballads and other songs. Two collections of such ballads and songs are mentioned and quoted in the Old Testament: the "Book of Jashar or Yashar[1]", from

[1] Yashar is possibly the same as Israel (Yishra-el) with, as we frequently find in Old Testament names, the Divine element *El* omitted. Accordingly the (Song) "Book of Yashar" is the (Song) "Book of Israel". See Peters, *Early Hebrew Story*, p. 5.

which, you remember, David's elegy over Saul and
Jonathan (2 Sam. i. 18) and Joshua's apostrophe to the
sun and moon (Josh. x. 12, 13) are quoted; and the
Book of the Wars of JEHOVAH, quoted in Num. xxi. 14.
These songs would doubtless be contemporary, or nearly
so, with the events they celebrate.   Nevertheless, as
sources of information as to bare matter of fact, they
would not have the value of the official records of the
later period.   The song would contain fact indeed, but
fact clothed in the glowing colours of lyric imagination.
It is probable that much of the history of the period
between the Exodus and the Davidic monarchy, is
simple song, i.e., poetry, rendered into prose.   We know
by the poetic quotations that it was so in some instances;
it was probably so generally.   If, in reading such books
as Joshua and Judges, we always bore in mind that what
we are reading is largely of the nature of a prose-poem,
it would relieve many of the difficulties we find in the
narrative.   (3) For a still earlier period the historian
would be dependent upon legend and myth.   The legend
would be still less trustworthy than the song, as a source
of information regarding matters of fact.   The legend,
as we have seen, contains a nucleus of fact, which can
sometimes be discovered by skilful questioning; but it
needs skilful questioning, and the result may sometimes
be disappointing.   From the myth, fact, as we have
seen, disappears altogether.   The value of the myth is
the value of the idea it embodies.   But we must
remember that facts themselves have value only as they
are significant, that is, as they embody ideas.   Such,
roughly, are the historical sources.   You see that as trustworthy evidences of matter of fact they vary amazingly.
We may compare the range of difference to that which

separates the responsible utterances of mature manhood
from the speech of childhood, unable, as yet, to distinguish between fact and fancy. This is true of all
history: the history of Greece, of Rome, our own
imperial history. Yet if we can still feel that, notwithstanding, we possess in our histories a substantially true
account of the course of development of the Greek, the
Roman, the British peoples, we need not hesitate to
believe that in Hebrew history we possess a like account
of the life of the Hebrew people. In reading the Hebrew
histories, however, we have an advantage we do not
always have in reading modern histories. The modern
historian studies, weighs and discriminates between his
authorities—sometimes perhaps with insufficient allow-
ance for personal equation, and then tells the story in
his own words. He seldom quotes his authorities at
length, but is content, for the most part, to refer to them
in brief footnotes. The Hebrew historian did his work
in a much more primitive fashion. He does not tell the
story in his own words, but, for the most part, transfers
his authorities bodily to his own pages, often contributing
nothing of his own save brief connecting sentences, and
often leaving conflicting authorities unreconciled. He
thus, much more directly than the modern historian,
brings us face to face with the original documents, so
that, as we have seen, we can even now distinguish
them. Accordingly, he brings us nearer to the times of
which he is writing than the modern historian brings us.
For example, J and E make us at once contemporaries
of the ninth and eighth centuries B.C., and still older
fragments embodied in those documents carry us back
even further.

Such, broadly, are the results which modern Criticism

claims to have reached. Their general effect is, as you can see, to assimilate the Hebrew literature, as far as its growth, development, and outward form are concerned, to the literatures of other peoples.

IV. But, that you may have the whole problem before you, I must now briefly direct your attention to another branch of modern study. Side by side with purely literary criticism, there have been proceeding researches in Archaeology and Anthropology. Prior to these researches Israel was the only branch of the Semitic race of which we had detailed knowledge, and knowledge derived from native sources. For knowledge of other Semitic peoples we were dependent upon fragmentary and obscure notices in the Classical authors. In such circumstances it was natural that Israel should be regarded as being wholly, and from the beginning, a unique people. Modern discovery in Egypt, Assyria, Babylonia, Phoenicia, Arabia, Palestine, compels us to modify this opinion, and to admit a much greater original likeness between Israel and the surrounding peoples, and the continuance of this likeness to a later period than we had formerly supposed[1].

We have now obtained, I trust, a substantially accurate view of the modern critical position. The question to which we must now address ourselves is just this: Can a people and a literature, of which this is the account, have been the vehicles of a Divine revelation? Can the writers of that literature have been the subjects of a Divine inspiration?

[1] See Buchanan Gray, *Divine Discipline of Israel*.

NOTE

TABLE OF DATES AND AUTHORSHIP

							B.C.
Ecclesiastes...	...	...	...	...	...	...	250
Daniel	...	...	...	...	...	...	167
Esther	...	...	...	...	...	...	150

(Taken from Prof. J. E. McFadyen's *Old Testament Criticism and the Christian Church.*)

It should be noted that the above dates are, for the most part, approximate only, and that regarding some of them there is still much uncertainty.

CHAPTER III

REVELATION AND INSPIRATION: WHAT THEY ARE NOT

In attempting to answer the question with which the preceding chapter closed, I must, in the first place, point out that Criticism, whether textual or historical ("higher"), does not itself answer this question. To give an account of the origin, structure, and history of a literature does not of itself determine the meaning and significance of that literature. That is determined by quite other considerations. The function of Criticism is entirely preparatory. It puts us, as far as may now be possible, in possession of the literature in its original form, as it came from the hands of its authors, freed from the corruptions and accretions of later ages; and it makes us acquainted (again, as far as may be) with the writers themselves, their environment and their methods of working. Having done this, Criticism's function ends. It is most important to bear in mind this limitation of Criticism's functions; it is often forgotten. I must now warn you against two errors, which have been, and still are, widely prevalent, and to which, I think, most of our difficulties are due. The first is the tendency to form *a priori* theories as to what a literature, professing to convey a Divine revelation, should be.

For example, if you have a theory that such a literature must have been verbally dictated by God ; must contain no admixture of the personality of the human penmen ; must contain no statements contrary to science—" that everchanging expression of imperfect human knowledge " ; no historical errors; no internal discrepancies ; that in course of transmission it must be miraculously guarded from all those errors of copyists to which ancient books in general are exposed : if, I say, you come to the examination of Biblical literature with these presuppositions, it is useless for me to proceed further. The Biblical literature does not fulfil these conditions. Men used to think that it did fulfil them. They said it must be so ; without more ado they declared that so it was. But Criticism, in both its branches, has shown that so it is not. It has shown that the Bible has not been verbally dictated by God. Even if this had been true of the original autographs, it is not true of our existing texts, which are the product of fallible human scholarship, weighing and selecting, from time to time, among various readings. It is true that, as we have seen, an overwhelming proportion of these various readings are entirely unimportant ; nevertheless, they make it impossible for us to be certain that, in every case, we have the exact words of Prophet or Apostle. Only the contemporary generations had these. If it were essential to a Divine revelation that it should be given in the very words of God, it were strange that the boon should have been confined to the immediate contemporaries of the writers. Further, it would seem to be certain that, if God be the immediate author of every word in the Bible, there could be no possibility of error or internal discrepancy ; yet, as we have seen (Chap. II), such there undoubtedly are. True, these are of trifling importance; still they would seem to be fatal to the theory of Divine dictation. Further, the Biblical writers themselves show by their method of quoting one another that they attached little importance to verbal accuracy. Thus, the New Testament writers make some two hundred and twenty-eight quotations from the Old Testament, and of these only fifty-three verbally agree with their originals. The vast majority of the quotations are taken not from the original Hebrew, but from the Greek Septuagint. Sometimes even where the Septuagint differs from the Hebrew, the former is quoted; sometimes the quotations agree with neither text. The New Testament writers evidently often depended upon memory, without troubling to turn to the written page, just as modern preachers often do. I may remark, in passing, that the more familiar one is with any book, the more likely one is, when quoting it, to trust to memory; it is only in the case of unfamiliar books that we are careful to verify our quotations. Now the most retentive memory is apt to err in the matter of strict verbal accuracy.

Again, the varieties of style exhibited by the Biblical writers are difficult to reconcile with the theory of Divine dictation. These variations of style are as marked as those of our English authors, and show, beyond dispute, that the individuality of the writers was not suppressed. Finally, the theory in question introduces hideous unreality into some of the most precious parts of Holy Scripture. The Psalter is a supreme collection of prayers, hymns, confessions of sin. Well; I ask, in the words of F. D. Maurice, " Is it possible that these " prayers, these songs, these confessions of sin, were

" repeated in the ears of a man that he might write them
" down for the good of the world? What! he did not
" actually pray, actually rejoice, actually confess! It is
" a deception throughout!... We shudder at the blas-
" phemy. Wherever the Psalmist learnt these words,
" they did come fresh and burning from his heart; they
" must; or how could they go fresh and burning into
" other men's hearts?" (*Sermons on the Prayer Book.*)

The phenomena, then, of the Biblical literature, as
disclosed to careful study, refute the *a priori* notion of
Divine dictation. But, perhaps, the Bible itself claims
this character. Now, we do indeed read from time to
time of "words of God"—" The word of the LORD came
to Isaiah"; and so on. But this is the simplest and
most obvious of metaphors in any language, and particularly in a language like the ancient Hebrew, so
concrete, pictorial, and unmetaphysical, for the communication of ideas or the quickening of thought in the
human mind: a metaphor all the more apt, since we
know as a fact of psychology that mental impressions
may be so strong as to take audible or visual form.
There are, so far as I remember, only two passages in
the Bible that speak of Divine agency in connexion
with the Bible as a whole, and neither of them involves
the theory of verbal dictation—(1) " Every scripture
" inspired of God is also profitable for teaching, for
" reproof, for correction, for instruction which is in
" righteousness: that the man of God may be complete,
" furnished completely unto every good work" (2 Tim.
iii. 16; R.V.). This is the only passage in which the
word "inspired" occurs, and you will observe that no
definition is given; nor is anything said about the
method, physical or psychical character, extent or limits,

of the inspiration. We are only told by what marks we may recognise an "inspired" writing; and these are not scientific or historical, but purely moral and spiritual: such a writing is profitable for instruction in righteousness, etc. The literal meaning of the word "inspired" *suggests* the being interpenetrated by, imbued with, the Divine Breath or Spirit, and so, the quickening of thought and action rather than the conveying of information. (2) "No prophecy of scripture is of private "interpretation. For no prophecy ever came by the will "of man: but men spake from God, being moved by the "Holy Ghost" (2 Pet. i. 20, 21; R.V.). I shall have occasion to return to this passage; here it suffices to say that there is no hint of verbal dictation; such is not at all the idea suggested by "moved, or borne along by the Spirit", "as a ship by the wind".

These are the only passages dealing with the inspiration of the Bible as a whole, or rather, to speak more accurately, with the inspiration of the Old Testament. They say nothing of the New Testament, of which they themselves are a part, and which, obviously, was not completed when they were being written.

The Bible, then, does not claim to have been verbally dictated, and gives no definition of inspiration. Neither does the authoritative teaching of the Catholic Church involve this theory, or furnish any definition. There is, so far as I am aware, only one statement upon this subject that can at all claim to be an authoritative expression of the mind of the Universal Church; and it is brevity itself. It is the clause in the Nicene Creed, "I believe in the Holy Ghost…Who spake by the prophets". It is evident that this clause simply affirms that prophetic men were the organs of a Divine message;

it says nothing as to what are, or must be, the characteristics of the writings in which the message is recorded.
In other words, all such questions are left open. From
this position our own Branch of the Catholic Church has
not deviated.

It, of course, accepts the Nicene statement. But,
when forced at the Reformation to re-define its position,
it contented itself with saying, " Holy Scripture con-
" taineth all things necessary to salvation; so that what-
" soever is not read therein, nor may be proved thereby,
" is not to be required of any man, that it should be
" believed as an article of the Faith, or be thought
" requisite or necessary to salvation ". It is evident that
here, likewise, all *a priori* theories and claims are put
aside; and further, that the Divine message contained
in the Bible is regarded as being concerned, not with
facts of science or natural history, but wholly with things
" necessary to salvation ", that is, the conditions by which
the soul of man can lay hold of, and live by, the power
and life of God. " The formularies of the Church ", says
Prof. Driver, " affirm, indeed, the Scriptures to be of
" supreme authority in matters of faith, they specify
" certain doctrines they declare to be contained in the
" Scriptures and to be the means of salvation; but they
" include no definition of inspiration; and while they
" define the books of which the Old Testament consists,
" they express no theory respecting either its literary
" structure, or the manner in which the Divine Will was
" communicated to its writers, or the stages by which,
" historically, revelation advanced ".

The Church's limitation of the scope of the Bible to
what is moral and spiritual is entirely in harmony with
what is said by the Biblical writers themselves. We

have seen that St Paul, when speaking of the Old Testament as a whole, finds its value in what is profitable for instruction in righteousness; as elsewhere, he says it has been written to inspire us with religious hope (Rom. xv. 4). So, too, the Psalmists, speaking of such portions of the Bible as were existing in their days, find their value in the moral and spiritual sphere :—

> "The law of the LORD is perfect, refreshing the soul:
> The testimony of the LORD is trustworthy, making
> wise the simple;
> The statutes of the LORD are right, rejoicing the
> heart;
> The commandment of the LORD is pure, enlightening
> the eyes" (Ps. xix. 7, 8).

The 119th Psalm again is one long celebration of this moral and spiritual power in such parts of the Divine Scriptures as were in existence in the Psalmist's day.

Modern Criticism, then, undoubtedly refuses to sustain the theory of verbal dictation and inerrancy; but, then, neither the Bible itself nor the authoritative creed of the Catholic Church puts forward such a claim. I now proceed to show that we are not entitled on grounds of reason to form either this or any other preconceived theory. I cannot better do this than by directing your attention to what Bishop Butler said more than one hundred and seventy years ago in the third chapter of the Second Part of *The Analogy*, entitled : "Of our Incapacity of judging what were to "be expected in a Revelation ; and the credibility, from "Analogy, that it must contain Things appearing liable "to Objections".

Butler's position is that *a priori* speculation as to

what God may, or may not, do is the most futile of
exercises. Nature is the work of God, and as such
reveals Him; yet "Nature is found to be greatly
" different from what, before experience, would have been
" expected; and such as, men fancy, there lie great objec-
" tions against". This, argues Butler, "renders it before-
" hand highly credible, that they may find the revealed
" dispensation likewise, if they judge of it as they do of
" the constitution of Nature, very different from expecta-
" tions formed beforehand, and liable, in appearance, to
" great objections". This observation Butler applies to
inspiration in particular. "We know not beforehand,
" what degree or kind of natural information it were to
" be expected God would afford men, each by his own
" reason and experience: nor how far he would enable
" and effectually dispose them to communicate it, what-
" ever it should be, to each other; nor whether the
" evidence of it would be certain, highly probable, or
" doubtful: nor whether it would be given with equal
" clearness and conviction to all. Nor could we guess,
" upon any good ground I mean, whether natural know-
" ledge, or even the faculty itself by which we are capable
" of attaining it, reason, would be given us at once, or
" gradually. In like manner, we are wholly ignorant
" what degree of new knowledge it were to be expected
" God would give mankind by revelation, upon sup-
" position of His affording one: or how far, or in what
" way, He would interpose miraculously, to qualify them,
" to whom He should originally make the revelation, for
" communicating the knowledge given by it; and to
" secure their doing it to the age in which they should
" live; and to secure its being transmitted to posterity.
" We are equally ignorant, whether the evidence of it

"would be certain, or highly probable, or doubtful; or
"whether all who should have any degree of instruction
"from it, and any degree of evidence of its truth, would
"have the same: or whether the scheme would be
"revealed at once, or unfolded gradually. Nay, we are
"not in any sort able to judge whether it were to have
"been expected, that the revelation should have been
"committed to writing; or left to be handed down, and
"consequently corrupted, by verbal tradition, and at
"length sunk under it, if mankind so pleased, and during
"such time as they are permitted, in the degree they
"evidently are, to act as they will.

  "But if it be said, 'that a revelation in some of the
"'above mentioned circumstances, one, for instance,
"'which was not committed to writing, would not have
"'answered its purpose', I ask, what purpose? It
"would not have answered all the purposes which it has
"now answered, and in the same degree; but it would have
"answered others, or the same in different degrees. And
"which of these were the purposes of God, and best fell
"in with His general government, we could not at all
"have determined beforehand....And thus we see, that
"the only question concerning...the authority of Scrip-
"ture (is), whether it be what it claims to be; not
"whether it be a book of such sort, and so promulgated,
"as weak men are apt to fancy a book containing a
"Divine revelation should. And therefore, neither ob-
"scurity, nor seeming inaccuracy of style, nor various
"readings, nor early disputes about the authors of
"particular parts, nor any other things of the like kind,
"though they had been much more considerable in
"degree than they are, could overthrow the authority of
"Scripture; unless the Prophets, Apostles, or our Lord

"had promised that the book containing the Divine
"revelation should be secure from those things ".

I have made this long quotation because I believe
the passage to be one of the most important ever written.
Dating from 1736, when as yet modern Criticism was in
its infancy, it is almost prophetic of the controversies
which were to be. Had it been attended to, those
controversies had never arisen, or at least been greatly
mitigated. We are not qualified to form *a priori* theories
of Revelation any more than of Nature. It was the
tendency to form such theories regarding Nature that
impeded the advance of the ancient world in the scientific
knowledge of Nature ; just as it has been the abandonment, since the time of Bacon, of such theorizing for the
more humble task of studying Nature as she is, that has
been the secret of the success of modern science.

Modern Criticism, so often accused of arrogance, has
clothed itself in a like humility, not daring to pronounce
what the Bible ought to be, but patiently trying to
discover what the Bible actually is ; and it is, I cannot
but think, being rewarded with a like success. But it
may be said—it has been said—that unless we have
some preconceived notion of what a Divine revelation
ought to be, we cannot recognise one when we see it ;
for recognition necessarily implies comparison with a
standard already present in the mind. Butler did not
overlook this difficulty. His answer was, that we were
entitled to make one presupposition, viz., that the alleged
revelation shall not violate the plain and unmistakable
laws of reason or of conscience. We cannot believe
what is contrary to reason, no matter what we wish, for
reason will not permit us. Nor can we accept as Divine
what is contrary to the elementary dictates of conscience,

for conscience itself is the gift of God: "Reason can, and it ought, to judge, not only of the meaning, but also of the morality of revelation". This presupposition, being negative, would not carry us very far. It would enable us to decide what was not a revelation, but not what was; that, Butler said, was determined by the evidence of miracles. This position of Butler's cannot, I venture to think, be regarded as wholly satisfactory. There are things in the Old Testament from which the modern conscience recoils, for example, the imprecatory Psalms; and to many minds to-day miracles, so far from being convincing proofs of a revelation, are themselves in need of convincing proof. The fact is, Butler, great as he was, was still the child of his age; he was entangled in a too *doctrinaire* conception of revelation. This is the second error against which I wish to warn you; for though Butler lived in the eighteenth century and we are living in the twentieth, the eighteenth century conception of revelation still widely prevails; it is, indeed, the conventional conception.

By a *doctrinaire* conception of revelation, I mean the conception of revelation as consisting in the supernatural communication to man of a body of mysterious truths otherwise inaccessible, and remaining, even when communicated, incapable of rational proof or of experimental verification[1]. If this be the view we hold, modern Criticism will, I fear, bring us into great straits. Uncertainties of text, doubts regarding authorship, the reality of miracle, may become serious things, when a purely verbal revelation is involved, the content of which is not self-evident to the reason or verifiable in ex-

[1] See Prof. W. A. Brown, *Christian Theology in Outline*, p. 45.

perience, but is dependent for its validity upon miraculous attestation[1].

Such a view of revelation may, perhaps, have
originated, as Prof. W. A. Brown suggests, in an attempt
to account for religious truths and practices inherited
from the past, whose origin and meaning men no longer
understood. That it should have persisted so long as an
account of the contents of the Bible, I can only ascribe
to mankind's faculty of imitation; whereby it comes
about that men take up opinions from one another,
and go on repeating them, generation after generation,
without subjecting them to any fresh and independent
investigation. For, surely, nothing can look more unlike
a compendium of abstract and incomprehensible truth
than the Old Testament. What is the main content of
the Old Testament? Is it not history and biography?
I have at hand an Old Testament containing 786 pages,
and of these 461 are historical and biographical. And
in this history and biography mundane affairs play no
inconspicuous part. Take, for example, the patriarchal
history. Is it not, in great part, occupied with such
things as marriages and births and deaths; flocks and
herds; journeyings and campings; lands and wells?
What abstract and incomprehensible truth do these
narratives contain? Nor does the character of the
history change when the patriarchal families have grown
into a nation. We still continue to read of very mundane doings: wars with their victories and defeats;
conquests; allotments of territory; laws; kings and

---

[1] I must not be understood as
depreciating "dogma", which I
believe to be inevitable and necessary. But the question is, whether
revelation is primarily and essentially
dogmatic, whatever dogma may be
legitimately deducted from it, when
once it has been given.

their doings; the rise and fall of dynasties. Truly a strange compendium of abstract truth, and marvellously unlike the books in which modern teachers are wont to convey such instruction.

If the Old Testament be a record of revelation, it may be confidently affirmed that revelation does not consist in the communication to man of a body of mysterious and unverifiable truths. I hope to suggest to you a quite different view of revelation : one which will show that revelation does not depend, for its recognition by us, upon its conformity with some preconceived standard in our minds; nor, for its verification, upon an accompaniment of miracle, but simply upon observation and experience.

CHAPTER IV

REVELATION AND INSPIRATION:
WHAT THEY ARE

WHAT, then, are Revelation and Inspiration? Revelation is God's Self-unveiling,—the manifestation of His character, mind, will, purpose. As such, revelation is living, concrete, personal, not theoretic and abstract; it is moreover continuous and universal: God is always and everywhere revealing Himself; not by words and syllables,—the Eternal is silent, "there is no speech nor language",—but in deed and act. No mere statements, though made by God Himself (if I may reverently say so), could really reveal Him. Personality cannot adequately be made known by words. Power, wisdom, justice, love, can only be revealed in *acts* of power, wisdom, justice, love. All God's Self-revelations are by acts: the great deeds of God are His Self-unveiling.

(1) Nature is a great act of God, an effect of which God is the ever-present Cause. As such, Nature reveals God; from it something can be learnt about Him. All effects are revelations of their causes.

(2) The moral nature of man is another revelation of God. Man has not created his own moral nature; it is a gift which he has received; it introduces him to a moral order which is above him, and which claims to rule him. In the things which his moral nature teaches him to approve and to condemn there is a revelation of God.

(3) History is a revelation of God. At first sight indeed it might seem as if history were only a revelation of man,—the unfolding upon the stage of time of what he has it in him to be, to do, and to devise. But further reflection shows that this is a superficial view of things, that there is another than the human factor in the stream of events. For what is it that most forcibly strikes the student of history? Is it not just this, that the ultimate issues of movements that seem to be initiated and carried forward by human agents, are so often other than—yes, and vaster than—the issues those human agents had in view, which latter are often mean and despicable enough? Something is manifestly going forward in human history and the movements of mankind that men have not devised; and yet something so truly of the nature of purpose as strongly to suggest a purposing and controlling mind. It is God. If it be said that the modifications of human purpose manifested in the course of history are simply due to the tough resistance of Nature, we must remember that, for the theist, Nature is but the instrument of God.

(4) There is one other revelation of God—the climax of all the others, to which they converge, and in which they find completion—viz., that given in Jesus Christ. But as our subject is the Old Testament, I shall not speak further of this supreme revelation, save to say

that it, like all others, is living, concrete, personal ; not
theoretic and abstract—

> "And so the Word had breath, and wrought
>   With human hands the creed of creeds
>   In loveliness of perfect deeds,
>   More strong than all poetic thought".

Such then are the Divine Self-revelations. In Nature,
in his own moral constitution, and in history, man is in
the presence of a Power, other than himself, which is
seeking to make Itself known to him, and which it is
his very life to know. And such revelation is continuous
and universal: God is always and everywhere manifesting
Himself to man. Revelation, so understood, requires
for its recognition by us no antecedent standard in our
minds, to which it conforms. It presents itself to us, as
any other objective fact presents itself. We feel that we
are in the presence of something other than ourselves,—
something which is manifesting itself. I have said that
this manifold Self-revealing of God is continuous and
universal; "Day unto day uttereth speech, and night
unto night showeth knowledge. Its voice is gone out
through all the earth". Yet not to all does it prove to
be a revelation. There is needed not only the objective
fact, but also the apprehending mind, able livingly to lay
hold on that which is presented to it. Not all have this
apprehending mind, or, if they have, some have it only
in rudimentary form. Multitudes have daily dealings
with Nature, yet see nothing divine in her ; she is for
them, as for brute creatures, simply a system of utilities
which ministers to their bodily needs. You remember
Wordsworth's lines :—

> "A primrose by the river's brim
>   A yellow primrose was to him ;
>   And it was nothing more".

On the other hand, Wordsworth himself was one to whom—

"— the meanest flower that blows can give
Thoughts that do often lie too deep for tears".

So, too, not all apprehend the revelation in man's moral nature. In many the moral nature is undeveloped; in many it is perverted and depraved: "Their hearts are waxed gross, and their ears heavy, and their eyes are shut".

Still more widespread, perhaps, is the failure to apprehend the Divine revelation in history. To multitudes history is simply a chaotic tumult of conflicting human wills,—a phantasmagoria of meaningless and aimless change.

Revelation is, in fact, an open secret. It is open; for it is spread before the eyes of all: it is secret; for not all can read it.

But some men have had the apprehending mind, in greater or less fulness of power, and to them Nature, man's moral constitution, history, have disclosed something of their inner, Divine meaning. These men—the Lawgivers, Priests, and Prophets, of the nations,—have been interpreters of the Divine Self-manifestations to their fellows. While such men have, probably, not been wanting in any nation, ancient Israel was unique in possessing a succession of them, continuing for ages, and of supreme endowment.

We thus come to the question of Inspiration. By Inspiration I understand the quickening and heightening of man's apprehensive powers by the Spirit of God, whereby he is enabled to apprehend the Divine revelation and to become an interpreter of it to his fellows. Inspiration is not the direct communication of knowledge to the human mind: it is the bestowal, or the quickening into life and energy, of man's power of insight, so that he perceives the Divine meaning in Nature or Conscience or History, which though always there and always appealing, had before been unperceived.

This view of Inspiration, as the energising of faculty, is entirely in harmony with the Biblical, particularly the Old Testament, teaching regarding the Spirit of God. In the Old Testament the word "Spirit" in general, whether applied to God or to man, has always the connotation of vitality, power, energy. This may be seen from such a passage as the following: " Now the " Egyptians are men, and not God ; and their horses " flesh, and not spirit" (Is. xxxi. 3). "Flesh is weak and " liable to decay; it has no inherent power in it; spirit " is power, or has power". "So, when it is said of the " Queen of Sheba that there was ' no more spirit ' in her " when she observed the wisdom of Solomon, it means " that she was overcome and felt weak".

In accordance with this conception of Spirit as power, any predominating determination or prevailing direction of the mind is called a *spirit* of such and such a kind. Hence one is of a *haughty* spirit, of a *humble* spirit, of a *steadfast* spirit, etc., that is, haughtiness, humility, steadfastness, is, in each case, the prevailing characteristic—the strong point, as we should say.

The usage is entirely the same as regards the Spirit of God. " The term expresses the fulness of vital power, the activities of vital energy." " The Spirit of God", as distinct (of course only in thought) from God Himself, " is God exerting power, God efficient, that is, actually exerting efficiency in any sphere". So, it is the Spirit of God that operates in the original creation and in the daily renewal of nature (Gen. i. 2; Ps. civ. 30). The effect of this operation of the Divine Spirit when man is the subject, is the quickening and heightening of man's powers, whether of body or mind or soul. So, in the Old Testament great bodily strength, exceptional intellectual power, deep stirrings of emotional life, are all ascribed to the Spirit of God. The man's personality is not depressed or effaced; on the contrary it is vitalised and raised to its highest power[1].

We are, then, in full accord with the uniform Biblical view of the Spirit of God, when we understand inspiration to mean the quickening and heightening of man's powers of spiritual insight. How the Divine Spirit thus operates on, and in, the spirit of men, it is impossible for us to determine. Inspiration is but a part of the larger problem of the whole relation of the Infinite to the finite.

We are likewise, I think, in harmony with the Biblical view when we say that the function of the man, so inspired, is to be the interpreter of the Divine Self-revelation. In a preceding lecture I quoted one of the very few passages that deal with this subject: " No prophecy " of scripture is of private interpretation. For no prophecy " ever came by the will of man: but men spake from God, " being moved—borne along—by the Holy Ghost". In this passage, which has figured largely in the Roman controversy, the phrase " of private interpretation " has been variously understood. But, to my mind, there is only one explanation that really satisfies the context. But, first, I must remind you that the term " prophecy " is not to be confined to the predictive portions of the

---

[1] See on the whole subject, Davidson, *Theology of the Old Testament*, pp. 117 ff.

Old Testament. The word has no time element in it at all. The prophet was not one who foretold, but one who spoke publicly for God—God's spokesman. That such speech for God might, and did, include prediction, is of course admitted ; but prediction is not of the essence of prophecy : he who declared what God had done in the past, or was doing in the present, was equally a prophet. Inspired preaching is the essential idea. The identification of prophecy with prediction is quite modern. Even as late as the seventeenth century it was still used in its wider and more accurate sense, as by Bishop Jeremy Taylor, who in his *Liberty of Prophesying* was not pleading for liberty to foretell, but for liberty to preach. In our passage St Peter may have had the predictive element in the Old Testament chiefly in mind; but his use of the term *prophecy* does not prove that he had. The point, however, is not very material to our present purpose. Rather, the crucial phrase in the passage is " of private interpretation ". I believe that the context is decisive : St Peter says that no prophetic Scripture springs from, arises out of, private interpretation. Prophetic Scripture is not the thing to be interpreted, as though it were obscure; on the contrary, St Peter calls it a " lamp shining in a dark place ". Prophetic Scripture is itself an interpretation of the mind and will of God. This interpretation, St Peter asserts not to be the offspring of the prophetic writers' own unaided powers, not the product of their own unaided fancy. Those writers were the subjects of a Divine influence, which lifted them above their own private fancies : " They spake from God, being borne along by the Holy Ghost ". It is because their interpretation thus springs from a Divine Source, that we

" do well to give heed to it as unto a lamp shining in a dark place ". The inspired writers, then, are interpreters of the Divine Self-revelation.

Let us now see the conclusions we have reached. Revelation is the Self-manifestation of God. This manifestation is not given in abstract propositions, but in concrete experience. It is God Himself—the God who ever lives and loves—revealing Himself in that manifold experience of ours, which we call Nature, Conscience, History. But, though that revelation is ever pressing upon us, not all of us clearly read its meaning, or find God in our experience. But some men are specially endowed to see what we do not see, and to interpret the revelation.

This Inspiration, then, is strictly correlative to revelation, as interpretation to the thing interpreted. It does not immediately communicate knowledge, much less knowledge upon all conceivable subjects. It is concerned with one factor in experience—the Divine. For we must remember that while the Divine is given in experience, yet in experience itself two factors are to be distinguished: (1) The Divine action; (2) The media through which the action takes place, the revelation is made; for example, in the case of Nature, matter—its forces and laws ; in the case of Conscience and History, human motive and action. Now the inspired man might have a clear vision of the Divine action, yet possess but imperfect knowledge of the media. In this latter respect his knowledge need not differ from that of his contemporaries. Indeed, we might almost say that it is in experience, as it presents itself to them, that they need to see the working of God, not in some ideal experience. Thus, it was in Nature, as she presented herself to men in the ninth century B.C., that the men of that century needed to see God; not as she presents herself to us, looking at her through the eyes of Copernicus, Newton, and the rest; whereas, of course, it is in this latter presentation of Nature that *we* require to see God. Had the inspired men of that far off age possessed our later knowledge, they would not have helped those early men to see God in Nature as they knew her.

Further, as the Divine revelation is continuous, the individual inspired man, confined, as he is, to a particular time and place, cannot have full knowledge even of the Divine revelation. He sees but a part, and therefore can know but in part. We must not, then, expect to find a complete interpretation of Divine revelation in any one inspired writer. This fragmentariness of the individual interpretation is explicitly recognised in the Bible. Thus, the Epistle to the Hebrews speaks of the ancient prophets as having received the Divine communication " in many parts and in many fashions ".

Further, there is no *a priori* reason for believing that all who were inspired in any degree were inspired in an equal degree, and possessed the same insight into things Divine. The inspiration, then, of the Biblical writers was confined to one interest—the Divine in experience and life. Outside that interest, they had no other Divine assistance in the exercise of their faculties than that normal co-operation which we all enjoy ; for, of course, all vitality and movement whatever depends upon the continuous co-operation of Him in Whom we live and move and are. Those faculties and that Divine co-operation, I have no doubt, they used faithfully, but they were not thereby, any more than other men, safe-guarded from error. This limitation of interest to the

Divine, is, as we have seen, the Bible's own account of itself. It is meant "to make us wise" indeed, but, "wise unto salvation".

This, then, is how I understand Revelation and Inspiration.

But, perhaps, this whole conception of a special inspiration of a few, is offensive to you. You say: The revelation is admittedly continuous and universal; why, then, is not the power of interpreting it, by which alone it becomes really revealing, equally continuous and universal,—the possession of each and of all? The difficulty is not one of theory but of fact; the fact is so, whatever be the explanation. But perhaps the solution is to be found in the word "universal". Revelation is given in experience. But experience is of two kinds: individual, and common or universal. Each of us has his own individual experiences, which he shares with no other; each of us shares in an experience which is common to many or to the race. Now these private experiences are also Divine revelations; and here, I think, each of us has, or may have, sufficient insight to understand their message. But the great common or universal experiences are beyond the power of ordinary individual insight. Here, the common run of men are dependent upon the exceptionally endowed man. They have enough of kinship with the Divine to recognise it when it is pointed out to them: they have not enough to make them original discoverers. The inspired man, then, deals with revelation as it has more than an in-dividual significance. This dependence upon the inspired man is only one instance of an interdependence which runs through all life. For example, we have not all, in anything like the same degree, the faculty of scientific discovery; but we can, most of us, appreciate the discoveries made by those who have the faculty. I could not discover for myself the law of gravitation; but when Newton discovers it, I may be able to appreciate it and use it for my practical guidance. And if we ask why we are thus interdependent; why each of us is not, in all respects, self-sufficing; we may answer: It is because the Divine ideal for man is not an individualistic, but a social, ideal. As we shall see later on, the goal of human history is a Divine-Human Society, whose members shall be united with one another and with God in a community of holy love and service. Interdependence, in the highest as well as in the lowest things, is one of God's methods of realising that end.

CHAPTER V

INSPIRATION—A FACT: BIBLICAL CONCEPTION
OF GOD

I PROCEED now to consider the question : Is inspiration, so defined, a fact? Have we any proof that the Biblical writers, or any of them, had a unique insight into the meaning of the Divine Self-manifestation? Now it is a fact that those writers of whom we have any detailed knowledge—Isaiah, Amos, Jeremiah, Ezekiel—did claim to have an inspiration from God. Thus, each of them had his "call" to the prophetic office. This call seemed to them to come with overwhelming force. None of them volunteered to be a prophet ; the *rôle* is forced upon him. He struggles against it, but in vain. But once he has submitted to his destiny, his language is entirely in harmony with the Divine Source of his inspiration. He speaks with authority, as one who *knows*, and does not merely guess and conjecture. This peculiar prophetic consciousness is an intensely interesting psychological phenomenon, which now that the religious consciousness in general has come to be counted worthy of serious psychological investigation, will, doubtless, receive the attention it deserves. Now, it is difficult to account for this belief of the prophets in

their own inspiration, otherwise than on the supposition
of its reality. Imposture is out of the question in the
case of men whose most marked characteristic was a
passion for righteousness. Nor does delusion seem a
more reasonable hypothesis in the case of a long succession of men,—men, too, in other respects, the sanest
of their day and generation. Nevertheless, it is not by
an analysis of the prophetic consciousness, of which we
can have but a very imperfect knowledge, that we try
to answer the question : Had they an inspired insight ?
But, rather, by asking a prior question : Had they a
true insight? Before we can decide that their insight
was inspired, we must know that it is true. This is the
only right method of procedure. Even the prophets'
own claim to be inspired must at last come to the test :
Had they, as a matter of fact, a true insight into things
Divine? And this we learn by observation and experience. Do we find them to be a lamp unto our feet
and light unto our path? I believe that we do find
them to be this ; and it is on this ground I believe them
to have been inspired, inspiration being the simplest,
and at the same time, an entirely adequate explanation
of the fact.

My task then is to try to show that in the Old
Testament we have, so far as it goes, a true interpretation of that manifold Self-manifestation of God in the
presence of which all men perpetually live.

And first, we must consider the Old Testament
conception of God. Here modern investigation, so far
from creating fresh difficulty, helps us to realize, more
vividly than ever before, the presence of a factor operating
in Hebrew thought and life which was not operative, at
least in anything like the same degree, among kindred

and surrounding peoples. We have seen that modern
investigation reveals a close original likeness between
Israel and the other branches of the Semitic family.
Now we know the general Semitic conception of deity.
The early Semites were neither monotheists nor poly-
theists, but, rather, monolatrous; that is, they believed
in the existence of many gods, but worshipped only
one. Each tribe or people had its own god whom it
worshipped; but each believed that the gods of other
tribes and peoples were equally real. This god was a
strictly national god; his realm was the territory occupied
by his worshippers; beyond that he had no jurisdiction.
The bond between him and his people was not ethical
and spiritual, but physical. His character was a reflection of his people's character; he was, we may say, the
national character or genius personified. He led his
people in war; was victorious in their victories, and
defeated in their defeats. If they were robbed of their
territory, so was he. If they were extinguished, he was
dethroned, and entered the ranks of the unemployed.
He might be angry with his people if they did not treat
him properly, and his anger might show itself in national
disaster—famine, pestilence, defeat; but he could not
afford, if he could help it, to allow them to be permanently worsted by their enemies. Beside this god
there stood a goddess, his female counterpart. Both
god and goddess had their material symbols. Such a
conception of deity had, manifestly, no ethical uplift.
A god who merely reflected the everyday character of
his people, presented no moral ideal to which they
might aspire. He might support the moral standard
already recognised by the community; but he could
contribute nothing to the elevation of that standard.

As a purely national deity, whose one concern was the power and prosperity of his own people, he, of course, knew nothing of intertribal or international morality. His people were at liberty to inflict the utmost damage upon their neighbours; indeed, the more they could aggrandise themselves at the expense of other peoples, the more the god was aggrandised. On the other hand, in the worship of this god there were two frightfully demoralising elements : (1) child sacrifice, of the practice of which in Canaan recent investigation has given us gruesome evidence, in the discovery, near an altar at Taanach and in the enclosure of the megalithic temple of Gezer, of jars containing the bones of children, and only of children[1]. (2) Licentiousness : Semitic temples had their troops of priests and priestesses consecrated to a life of shame. This was a marked feature both of Canaanite and Babylonian worship.

Such then was the early Semitic conception of the Divine, in which, together with the other branches of the same stock, the Hebrew people shared.

Now contrast with this the conception reached by the Prophets of Israel. Of course, for the full Biblical conception we must include the New Testament, but even within the Old Testament the contrast is amazing. On the one hand, we have a purely local and tribal deity, whose jurisdiction and whose interests are limited to one small people and one small spot of earth,— one among a multitude of equally petty gods ; whose character is but a reflection of that of his worshippers,— without fixed—still less, lofty—moral content; a god who is symbolised by material and often obscene symbols, and whose worship is materialistic, cruel, licentious. On

---

[1] Peters, *Early Hebrew Story.*

the other hand, we have "the high and lofty One that inhabiteth eternity, Whose name is Holy"; Sole, "beside whom is none else"; the Creator and Sustainer of the universe, "measuring the waters in the hollow of His hand, and meting out the heavens with a span"; wholly spiritual, Who may not, without sin, be symbolised by any created thing or any "gravure of art and man's device"; Whose character is unchangeable, and unchangeably righteous, "He is not a man that He should lie, nor a son of man that He should repent", "Whose righteousness is like the strong mountains". And yet, He is loving and merciful too, and His love and mercy know no limits of time or space:—"They endure for ever"; "They are over all His works". He has, indeed, chosen Israel, but it is "that it may bring His salvation unto the ends of the earth". Nor must Israel dream that this Divine choice means favouritism, or exempts it from the moral action of retributive law; nay, privilege means increased responsibility: "You only have I known "of all the peoples of the earth; *therefore* I will punish "your iniquities" (Amos iii. 2). And what is the worship in which He delights, and who may draw near to Him? Not material sacrifice however costly, even though it be that of the firstborn child: "Wherewith shall I come "before the LORD, and bow myself before the high God? "Shall I come before Him with burnt offerings, with "calves of a year old? Will the LORD be pleased with "thousands of rams, or with ten thousands of rivers of "oil? Shall I give my firstborn for my transgression, "the fruit of my body for the sin of my soul? He hath "showed thee, O man, what is good; and what doth the "LORD require of thee, but to do justly, and to love "mercy, and to walk humbly with thy God"? "The

" sacrifices of God are a broken spirit : a broken and a
" contrite heart, O God, Thou wilt not despise ";

> "LORD, who shall abide in Thy tabernacle?
> Who shall dwell in Thy holy hill?
> He that walketh uprightly, and worketh righteousness;
> He that speaketh the truth in his heart,
> He that backbiteth not with his tongue,
> Nor doeth evil to his neighbour,
> Nor taketh up a reproach against his neighbour,
> In whose eyes a vile person is contemned;
> But he honoureth them that fear the LORD.
> He that sweareth to his own hurt, and changeth not.
> He that putteth not out his money to usury,
> Nor taketh a bribe against the innocent" (Ps. xv.).

It is a worship in which religion and morality are
indissolubly blended, and duty to man is made the
conditio sine qua non of acceptable service of God.

Such then is the conception of God and His require-
ment to which Israel attained, and Israel alone. No
kindred people attained it ; nor indeed has any people
ancient or modern wholly attained it, who has not come
within the sphere of Israel's influence.

Regarding this conception two questions may be
asked : (1) How did Israel attain it? (2) Is the conception a true account of that mysterious Power, other
than man himself, in whose presence man instinctively
feels himself to be?

(1) Can we say in answer to the first question that
the conception was a natural evolution in course of time
out of that primitive conception of deity, which, as we
have seen, early Israel shared with his Semitic brethren ?
Many, probably, in our day would give this account of
the matter ; but I do not think it can be regarded as
adequate. And for this reason. Evolution is the un-

folding of a germ in which the last result is potentially
present from the first : the oak is potentially present in
the acorn, and from an acorn you can, by evolution, get
nothing but an oak; type is preserved throughout.
Now, from monolatry monotheism might conceivably be
naturally evolved : worship of one god might naturally
pass into belief in one god. But how could a deity
delighting in cruelty and lust naturally develop into
One Whose mercy is everlasting and Who is "of purer
eyes than to behold iniquity"? There seems to be here
a difference in kind,—the introduction of a new and
contradictory element, not present in the original germ.
Moreover, if it were all a purely natural evolution, why
did not a like evolution take place among the kindred
peoples? They were of the same stock with Israel, and
their environment was not widely dissimilar.

But, if not evolution, was it, perhaps, the progress of
civilisation? In reply, it may be pointed out that Israel
was not by any means the first of the Semitic peoples
to attain civilisation. The Babylonians had attained a
splendid civilisation ages before Israel appears on the
stage of history. The recently discovered Code of Hammurabi shows that in his age (circ. 2250 B.C.) Babylonia
had attained a high degree of civilisation. "Law and
"justice had reached an extremely advanced stage of
"development. It (the code) presupposes regularly in-
"stituted courts of justice with duly qualified judges, and
"it requires us to conclude, further, that this stage had
"long been in existence" (S. A. Cook, *Laws of Moses and
the Code of Hammurabi*, p. 48). Now if we may trust
the identification of Hammurabi with the Amraphel
mentioned in Gen. xiv. 1, the Babylonian king was a
contemporary of Abraham. Further, when the Semitic

Babylonians made themselves masters of Babylonia (circ. 2800 B.C.) they inherited from the conquered people a civilisation which can be traced back to 7000 B.C., and which included, among other things, the art of writing. Yet this advanced civilisation did not avail to cleanse Semitic Babylonian worship of its licentiousness. The Canaanites too were a highly civilised people at the time of the Hebrew conquest, yet their worship likewise remained licentious. But, indeed, whatever other virtues civilisation is favourable to, and doubtless to many virtues it is favourable, it is gravely questionable whether it is specially favourable to the virtue of purity. It was not so in ancient Greece or Rome ; who shall say that it is so even in modern Christendom ?

But, perhaps, Israel's ethical monotheism was due to Israel's peculiar genius? Now apart from the fact that the word "genius" explains nothing, but is only another way of stating the fact to be explained, the records forbid us to think that Israel, as a people, had any special bent towards ethical monotheism. The records show that, down to the Captivity, the pagan Semitism, in its grossest features, more or less prevailed, sometimes rather more than less. In the popular thought JEHOVAH was still a national God, and the popular worship was materialistic, cruel, and licentious. It was precisely against this paganism, with its consequent moral corruption, that the great prophets protested. It was to the persistence of this paganism that they attributed the final catastrophe of the nation[1]. I hold that neither evolution, nor civilisation, nor national genius, will explain Israel's ethical monotheism. The fact is, it was the achievement of certain great personalities—a Moses,

[1] See 2 Kings xxii.

an Elijah, an Amos, an Isaiah, a Jeremiah, an Ezekiel.
In these democratic days we are apt to underrate the
part played by personality in human progress. We are
apt to think that the human race, like a flock of birds,
rises simultaneously in all its parts. But in truth it is
not so. "The progress of the world has been achieved
"chiefly through great men, more than mere products of
"their times and of previous conditions, who stand out
"from all that has gone before or that surrounds, in such
"a way that they seem to be rather a contradiction than
"a result of their antecedents and their surroundings".
It is probably because our own age is so lamentably
lacking in great men, and mediocrity reigns in every
sphere, that the modern world finds itself struggling with
problems—religious, political, social—which it cannot
solve. Be this as it may, Israel undoubtedly owed her
religious and ethical pre-eminence to a succession of
great personalities. Just why Israel alone of Semitic
peoples, alone, may we not say of all peoples, had this
succession of great men—great in this one sphere of
ethical religion,—is an urgent question for those who
take a naturalistic view of things. One or two such
personalities would not seem so strange; it is a succession
of them extending through several centuries that is the
puzzling thing. The Old Testament, as you know, gives
a quite adequate account of the phenomenon: these
men were raised up by God. Is there any other account
equally adequate? When and with whom this ethical
and monotheistic conception of God began, modern
Criticism leaves in some doubt. Our traditional view
was that it began with Abraham, "the father of them
that believe". Many modern scholars think that Moses
was the great initiator and innovator. Other "more

advanced" scholars give the honour to the Prophets of the eighth century—Amos, Hosea, Isaiah, Micah. It is after all a subordinate question. The important thing is, that it *did* begin, and that, once begun, it went on till it reached that lofty, yet not cold and abstract, but rich and full and warm ethical monotheism which we sketched earlier in this lecture. If, where experts differ, one may venture upon an opinion, I should say that the indications point back at least to Moses. Moses may not have attained to full monotheism : he may have been only monolatrous ; other gods may have had existence for him, while he worshipped JEHOVAH alone. But this one great step at least had been taken by him : no goddess[1] stands beside the God of Moses; JEHOVAH is a God of purity. We stand on surer historical ground with Elijah, who, with his loud laughter at the absurdities of Baal-worship, resists, single-handed, the attempt of the Tyrian Jezebel to make the cruel and licentious worship of the Tyrian Baal the state religion of Israel. With the prophets of the eighth century, it is agreed, ethical monotheism has been achieved. But how did these prophetic men themselves gain this conception? Well ; as we have seen, they did not get it from their antecedents or their surroundings. Nor is there any evidence that they reached it by any process of reasoning. The Hebrew mind was non-speculative ; nor is there any trace of speculation on the Being of God in the prophetic writings which have come down to us. Their own account is that it came to them unsought ; it *found* them. It was an intuition, a beholding with the eye of

---

[1] So fundamental is this trait in the religion of Israel that " the Hebrew language is not even com- petent to form the word 'goddess'." —See Cornill's *Prophets of Israel*, p. 23.

the soul, of something which the mind did not create, but which it saw. What Isaiah, in splendid symbolism, tells us of his own experience, they all tell us, in some form or other. " I saw also the Lord sitting upon a "throne, high and lifted up, and His train filled the "temple. Above it stood the seraphim : each one had "six wings; with twain he covered his face, and with "twain he covered his feet, and with twain he did fly. "And one cried unto another and said, Holy, holy, holy "is the LORD of Hosts, the whole earth is full of His "glory. And the foundations of the thresholds were "moved at the voice of him that cried ". This I hold to be the simplest, most reasonable account of the matter. Ethical monotheism was always true : God was always One, and always Holy. In Him men were living and moving and having their being ; He was always presenting Himself to them, always manifesting Himself. Men were dimly conscious of His presence ; they felt that there was some Being, other than themselves, with whom they had to do. But they did not truly read the revelation ; their eyes were dim, their hearts were gross ; they pictured Him to themselves in their own worst image. To the Prophets of Israel was given by Divine inspiration the apprehending mind. They truly read the open secret of Divine Being, and became interpreters of it to the world.

(2) But did they truly read it ? I believe that only experience can answer this question. Their conception of God as One, spiritual, perfectly good, creating, sustaining and ordering all things in holy love, commends itself, indeed, to our conscience and heart and reason, as worthy of all acceptation. But whether what we subjectively approve is also objectively valid, can only be

decided by experience of its working. This is true of all our conceptions of external reality. The truth of all such conceptions—their correspondence with reality—can be reached by no mere process of reasoning—that may make them seem probable—but only by experience. Let us consider this a little more closely. Life is the resultant of the interaction between personality and environment. If we are in right and true relations with environment, life will be vigorous and full; if we are in wrong and false relations, life will be poor and feeble, and may even be destroyed. We have a threefold life—physical, moral, spiritual. Corresponding with this triple life, our environment is likewise threefold; we live in the midst of a physical, a moral, a spiritual environment—physical nature, human society, God. A rich and full human life depends upon our being in right and true relations with all three. Thus, if I am in right relations with physical nature, I shall be physically healthy; if I am in right relations with human society, I shall be morally healthy; if I am in right relations with God, I shall be spiritually healthy. Of this threefold environment, the last—the spiritual—is the highest, and, in the last analysis, it includes the other two: both physical nature and human society have their being in and from God. Now the proof that I am in right relations with this environment consists in no elaborate process of reasoning, but simply in experience. For example, it is the experience of health or disease, and not any elaborate argument, which tells me whether I am in right relations with physical nature or not.

But man is a rational being, that is, a being whose life is governed by conceptions. Accordingly the quality of his life depends upon the conceptions he forms of his

environment. If he have right conceptions of his environment, and act upon them, his life will be healthy and
full; if he have wrong conceptions and act upon them,
life will be diminished in volume and may be destroyed;
for example, if his conception of such elements of his
physical environment as fire and water, does not include
the fact that they can burn and drown, his life is all too
likely to come to a speedy end. Accordingly the truth
or falsehood of his conceptions of his environment is
conclusively proved by the result, that is, by experience.
If I am physically healthy, my conceptions of my
physical environment must be substantially true; if I am
morally healthy, my conceptions of my social environment must likewise be substantially true. And precisely
the same holds good of the spiritual environment. If I
am spiritually healthy, my conceptions of my spiritual
environment must be substantially true. The question
then as to the validity of the Biblical conception of
God, that is, of man's spiritual environment, is simply
a question of experience. Do those who accept that
conception, *and act upon it*, find that it augments life,
that it helps them to realise life's best possibilities? If
they do, if multitudes of men in all ages have found
it so, then that conception is substantially in accord
with Ultimate Reality, that is, it is substantially true[1].
I believe that experience answers this question in the
affirmative. I believe that experience shows that,
whether by special inspiration or not, the Biblical writers
attained a true apprehension of the Divine Nature and
Character.

[1] From this point of view Agnosticism is an irrelevance.

CHAPTER VI

BIBLICAL INTERPRETATION OF THE SELF-MANIFESTATION OF GOD IN NATURE

WE have now to see how the Biblical writers interpret the Self-manifestation of God in Nature, in Man's Moral Constitution and in History.

And, first, in Nature. We turn to the opening chapters of Genesis. According to modern Criticism these chapters are the work of different authors and belong to different ages. We have, in fact, two cosmogonies, or portions of two cosmogonies, placed side by side by the final editors or compilers of Genesis: Gen. i.—ii. 3 being one cosmogony, and Gen. ii. 4 ff. being another, or fragment of another, and quite distinct, cosmogony. Of these cosmogonies the second is by far the earlier, and is assigned to the document J (see ch. ii.), the first being assigned to P. Some of the grounds upon which this distinction of authorship and age is based are easily understood. Thus, there is a difference in the Divine names used in the two cosmogonies,—in Gen. i.—ii. 3, "God" (ELOHIM) being used, while in Gen. ii. 4 ff. we find "LORD God" (JEHOVAH-Elohim)[1].

[1] This combination of Divine names is peculiar. Probably JEHOVAH alone is original, Elohim being added by a later hand, under the influence of the later superstition regarding the use of the Divine Proper Name. Elohim is thus meant to be read not along with, but instead of, JEHOVAH. See *infra* ch. ix. The combination occurs in only five other passages in the whole Old Testament (Ex. ix. 30; 2 Sam. vii. 22, 25; 1 Chron. xvii. 16 sq.; 2 Chron. vi. 41 sq.; Ps. lxxxiv. 9, 12 *Heb.*).

Then, there is very plainly a difference of style, the later account being severe, restrained, lofty, rhythmical, and marked at intervals by the refrain—" And God saw that it was good " : while the earlier is easy, flowing, pictorial. But the most striking difference is in the representation of the creative process. In the earlier account the Divine activity is represented in the most naïvely anthropomorphic way : God " forms " man out of clay as a potter would ; He " breathes " into man's nostrils ; He " plants " a garden ; He " brings " the animals to man ; He "builds" (R.V. marg.) a woman. In the later account anthropomorphism is reduced almost to a vanishing point. God speaks indeed, and that is human, but His word has effects no human voice could have,—" He spake and it was done ". There are other differences of representation : the framework of days, so prominent in the later, is absent from the earlier account ; so, too, in this, man is centre ; in that, he is crown.

The naïve anthropomorphism marks Gen. ii. 4 ff. as being the earlier account. Now where, if anywhere, are we to look in these chapters for evidence of special inspiration ? As you are aware, until quite recently it was the custom to regard the whole narrative, and all its details, as the direct product of inspiration. It was a simple theory ; but it can no longer be maintained ; not only because some of the details conflict with some of the most assured results of scientific investigation, but also because similarities exist between the Biblical cosmogony and certain other more ancient cosmogonies, of such a kind as at least to suggest that the Biblical writers were acquainted with, and drew upon, already existing material. The cosmogony, which, in this connexion, is of most importance for our purpose is the

Assyrio-Babylonian, of which I now proceed to give some account. Scholars have long been acquainted with some details of this cosmogony, preserved in extracts from the writings of Berossus, a contemporary of Alexander the Great and a priest of Bel in Babylon, and in Damascius, a Neo-Platonic philosopher of the sixth century A.D. But we are now happily in a position to supplement and correct these fragmentary notices by the aid of much fuller and more ancient material. Between 1872 and 1876 the late George Smith discovered among the ruins of the library of Asshurbanipal (668–626 B.C.) at Nineveh portions of a series of tablets, written in the cuneiform character, which proved to contain the Babylonian account of the Creation. These tablets were written in the seventh century B.C., but their contents are regarded by Assyriologists as going back, in all probability, to the twenty-second or twenty-third century. Other portions have been discovered since Smith's time, but we do not even now possess the complete series, and what we do possess is very imperfect, the tablets being broken and in parts indecipherable[1].

The following account of the cosmogony is taken from Professor Driver's *Commentary on Genesis.* "It is a kind of epic poem, the theme of which is the glorification of Marduk, the supreme god of Babylon, declaring, how, after a severe conflict, he had overcome the powers of chaos and darkness, and had so been enabled to create a world of light and order. The first tablet (of which only a fragment is preserved) describes how, before what we call heaven and earth came into being, there existed a primeval watery chaos (*Tiāmat,*

[1] Mr L. W. King, of the British Museum, has published a beautiful edition entitled *The Seven Tablets of Creation.*

corresponding to the Hebrew *Tehōm*, the 'deep' of Gen. i. 2), out of which the Babylonian gods were evolved :—

> When above the heaven was not yet named,
> And the land beneath yet bare no name,
> And the primeval Apsu (the abyss), their begetter,
> And Chaos (?), Tiāmat, the mother of them both—
> Their waters were mingled together,
> And no field was formed, no marsh was to be seen ;
> When of the gods still none had been produced,
> No name had yet been named, no destiny fixed ;
> Then were created the gods in the midst of [heaven?]
> Lachmu and Lachamu were produced,
> Long ages passed...
> Anshar and Kishar were created, and over them...
> Long were the days, then there came forth...
> Anu, their son...
> Anshar and Anu...
> Ea, whom his fathers, his begetters...

" The subsequent parts of the first tablet describe how Apsu, disturbed at finding his domain invaded by the new gods, induced Tiāmat to join with him in contesting their supremacy ; he was, however, subdued by Ea ; and Tiāmat, left to carry on the struggle alone, provided herself with a brood of strange and hideous allies.

" The second, third and fourth tablets, describe how the gods, alarmed at Tiāmat's preparations, having taken counsel together, appointed Marduk as their champion, and how Marduk equips himself with winds and lightnings for the fray. The account of the combat, in the fourth tablet, is told with dramatic force and vividness. Armed with his weapons Marduk advances, he seizes Tiāmat in a huge net, and transfixes her with his scimitar. The carcase of the monster he splits into

halves, one of which he fixes on high, to form a firma-
ment supporting the waters above it :—

> He cleft her like a flat (?) fish into two parts,
> The one half of her he set up, and made a covering for
>   the heaven,
> Set a bar before it, stationed a guard,
> Commanded them not to let its waters issue forth.
> He marched through the heaven, surveyed the regions
>   thereof,
> Stood in front of the abyss, the abode of the god Ea.
> Thus Bel measured the structure of the abyss,
> A great house, a copy of it, he founded E-sharra ;
> The great house E-sharra which he built as the heaven,
> He made Anu, Bel, and Ea, to inhabit as their city.

" The fifth tablet (still incomplete) describes the
formation of the sun and moon, and afterwards the
appointment of the years and months :—

> He made the stations for the great gods,
> As stars resembling them he fixed the signs of the zodiac,
> He ordained the year, defined divisions,
> Twelve months with stars, three each, he appointed.
> After he had...the days of the year...images,
> He fixed the station of Nibir (Jupiter), to determine their
>   limits,
> That none (of the days) might err, none make a mistake.
> The station of Bel and Ea, he fixed by his (Jupiter's) side.
> *   *   *   *   *   *   *   *
> He caused the moon-god to shine forth, entrusted to him
>   the night ;
> Appointed him as a night-body to determine the days.

" The opening lines of tablet vii., where Marduk is
hailed as 'Bestower of planting', show that the poem
mentioned the creation of vegetation; and it is probable
that this was mentioned in the lost parts of tablet v.

The sixth tablet describes the creation of man :—

When Marduk heard the word of the gods,
His heart prompted him, and he devised (a cunning plan).
He opened his mouth, and unto Ea (he spake),
(That which) he had conceived in his heart he imparted
    (unto him) :
My blood will I take, and bone will I fashion,
I will make man, that man may...
I will create man who shall inhabit (the earth?),
That the service of the gods may be established, and that
    (their) shrines (may be built).

"The seventh tablet consists of a hymn, addressed by the gods to Marduk, celebrating his deeds and character, representing him as all-powerful, beneficent, compassionate, and just."

I have given the Babylonian cosmogony with some fulness of detail, because it is only as we have ourselves some knowledge of it, that we can *feel* alike the similarities and the contrasts which it presents to the Biblical narrative. For it does present similarities. "The out-"line, or general course of events", says Professor Driver, "is the same in the two narratives. There are in both "the same abyss of waters at the beginning, denoted by "almost the same word, the separation of this abyss "afterwards into an upper and a lower ocean, the forma-"tion of heavenly bodies, and their appointment as "measures of time, and the creation of man". Many modern scholars—probably the great majority—hold that these similarities cannot be explained as mere coincidences. They suggest some kind of mutual connexion, though just what the connexion is, is a matter of dispute. Some scholars think that the Hebrew people gained a knowledge of the Babylonian cosmogony from

the Canaanites. It is now known that from about
3000 B.C. onward there existed a fairly close political
connexion between Babylonia and Palestine, and that
Babylonian civilisation, culture, and religion gradually
extended westward to the Mediterranean. The Tel
el-Amarna tablets (circ. 1400 B.C., discovered in 1887)
show that so completely did Babylonian influence
dominate Canaan 150 years after Babylonian rule
had given way to Egyptian, that the language and
script of official intercourse between Canaan and
Egypt still continued to be the Babylonian cuneiform[1].
Accordingly it is thought that the Canaanites had
adopted the Babylonian cosmogony, and that thus the
Hebrews became acquainted with it. Other scholars
carry the connexion much further back in time, and
think that the similarities are best explained as due
to " a common inheritance which has been variously
developed and used by Israel and the Babylonians " (so
Dillmann). The point, for our purpose, is of little importance. But far greater than the similarities is the
difference between the two cosmogonies. The difference
lies in their respective theological conceptions, and it is
profound. The Babylonian cosmogony is dominated by
" an exuberant and grotesque polytheism ", to a far
greater extent than the extracts given above indicate.
Chaos is anterior to deity, the gods emerge, or are
evolved out of it, and Marduk gains his supremacy only
after a long contest. The other is marked by a severe
and lofty monotheism. There is but one God, and He
truly creates ; chaotic matter has no prior independent
existence ; it and all its potentialities are called into
existence by His Sovereign will ; He wages no uncertain

[1] See Peters, *Early Hebrew Story*, pp. 30 ff.

conflict; He is supreme and absolute from the first: " In the beginning He created the heavens and the earth ".

We are now able to see where we are to look for evidences of inspiration in the Biblical writer. Plainly not in the order in which the creation process is arranged. That order had been outlined ages before his time. Nor indeed was special Divine assistance at any time required for the perception of this order. If without special inspiration man is able to-day to give the minute and elaborate account of the order of the universe that modern science gives, he was able, as soon as he became intelligent enough to enquire at all, to perceive the simple order of the Genesis cosmogony. That order is simply the order suggested to intelligent non-scientific observation. Man must early have observed the mutual relations and interdependence that prevail in the world ; how that human life depends upon, and presupposes, animals and plants ; these, again, land and water ; while light is the pre-condition of all life and order. And this is just the order in Gen. i.—ii. 3—light, water, land, vegetation, animals, man. A special Divine revelation was not needed to teach men this sequence ; the Biblical writers do not claim such aid ; the Babylonian cosmogony would seem to show that they did not receive it.

What is special and peculiar to the Biblical writers is their sublime doctrine of Creation,—that all these things, and the whole universe, owe their being to the free, intelligent, deliberate, sovereign will and operation of one personal God. For this, we must remember, is what we mean by creative action, in contrast with other forms of action. The process may be instantaneous ; it

may be spread over ages; it may be continuous and
eternal; but, provided it is free, sovereign, intelligent,
it is still creative.   The writer of Gen. i.—ii. 3 seems to
confine the process within the limits of one week; but
apart from the Fourth Commandment (as given in
Exodus xx. not as given in Deut. v.) this representation
is not referred to elsewhere in the Old Testament.   Even
Ps. civ., which in other respects follows Gen. i.—ii. 3 so
closely, makes no suggestion of the seven days; indeed,
in this particular, the Psalmist seems to have taken
another view, since he passes from the creation of the
universe to its continuous maintenance by God, without
such a break as is implied by the seventh day of Genesis.
Indeed already in Gen. ii. 4 ff. another representation
of the creative process is given; and yet others in Job
xxvi. 7—10; xxxviii. 4 ff.; Ps. xxiv. 2; Prov. viii. 24 ff.
As Dillmann says, "with reference to the particulars
" of the process we find no fixed doctrine among the
"ancient (Hebrew) nation during the period of intellectual
" freedom, but divergences, according to individual ways
" of thinking, or the state of attainment, for the time
" being, in physical science".   And in early days the
same freedom obtained in the Christian Church.   Such
Christian thinkers as Origen and St Augustine do not
seem to have felt themselves precluded by anything in
Genesis from freely speculating as to the creative process.
Thus, Origen held the doctrine of eternal creation,—
that " God's eternal existence was always accompanied
by a universe in some stage of being".   Augustine
regarded creation as covering long periods of time.   It
was not until comparatively recent times, when the
theory of verbal inspiration came into vogue, that the
acceptance of the representation in Gen. i.—ii. 3 came

to be regarded as an obligation of faith. But, though prevalent in the Church, this view never received dogmatic authorisation, the Church in her corporate capacity being content with the general affirmation of God's creative action contained in the Catholic creed—"I "believe in one God the Father Almighty, Maker of "heaven and earth, and of all things visible and in-"visible",—an affirmation which manifestly leaves the question of method and duration perfectly open. But, with whatever variety of representation, the Biblical writers are constant as to the fact of creation—that the entire universe, visible and invisible, owes its existence to the free, intelligent, deliberate, sovereign will and operation of one personal God. This is the specifically Biblical contribution to our knowledge of the universe in which we dwell. And it is in this doctrine that evidence of inspiration is to be found. This doctrine, so far as I know, is peculiar to the Biblical writers. They did not receive it from any outside source. They were familiar, as we have seen, with the Babylonian belief; but this belief contains no real doctrine of creation,—the gods themselves were evolved out of chaos. They might also have been familiar with Egyptian speculation,—but neither does this give a doctrine of creation. Egyptian speculation was pantheistic,—it saw in matter but the varying forms and manifestations of an omnipresent Divinity. In later ages they might have learnt something of the Greek view of the universe. But this also was lacking in a doctrine of creation. Greek speculation was either pantheistic or dualistic: God was conceived as simply present in the world as its animating principle; or, matter is regarded as an independent reality over against God, "who is ever striving to fashion it

"into ideal forms, but who is never able wholly to over-
"come its resistance". Indeed, I think it is true to say
that outside the Biblical sphere of influence no full
doctrine of creation has ever been attained. The human
mind has oscillated between pantheism and dualism.
Of pantheism it may be enough to say that it destroys
the human will, which must be conceived as *other*
than the Divine Will, and with the human will the
possibility of morality disappears. Moreover, however
persons of poetic temperament may succeed in holding
a spiritual pantheism, in the popular mind pantheism
has a fatal tendency to become mere materialism ; and
materialism is almost demonstrably false. Of dualism
it may be said that, by postulating some eternal principle
existing independently of God, it shatters the unity of
the universe ; and the unity of the universe is one of
the first principles of science.

Following upon the Biblical doctrine of creation,
comes the Biblical doctrine that God continuously sus-
tains, and sovereignly controls, the universe He has
created. This doctrine depends upon the doctrine of
creation, and is indeed what makes the doctrine of
creation practically important. We might be content
to leave the origin of the universe an open question, if
we could be sure that, now that it exists, it is wholly
controlled by the God of righteousness and love. But
with its origin a still open question, this is just what we
cannot be sure of. If there be anything in the universe
that does not owe its existence to God, anything that
possesses qualities and powers of its own which He
did not conceive and bestow, that thing limits His
sovereignty. Only One Who sovereignly creates can
sovereignly control. Hence the Bible has a fuller and

grander doctrine of Divine sovereignty over the universe
than we find elsewhere:

> "The LORD reigneth; He is apparelled with majesty;
> The LORD is apparelled; He hath girded Himself with
>   strength:
> The world also is stablished that it cannot be moved.
> Thy throne is established of old:
> Thou art from everlasting.
> The floods have lifted up, O LORD,
> The floods have lifted up their voice;
> The floods lift up their waves.
> Above the voices of many waters,
> The mighty breakers of the sea,
> The LORD on high is mighty." (Ps. xciii.)

But I need not quote; the Bible is full of the thought of
the absolute sovereignty of God over the whole created
universe.

The third Biblical doctrine is that Nature has been
created and is controlled for moral and spiritual ends.
The material universe is not an end in itself; it is a
means to an end. That end is the realisation of the
kingdom of God,—a community of moral and spiritual
beings like to God Himself, and living in union with
Him and with one another, in a fellowship of holy love
and service (see pp. 149 ff.). Of this moral and spiritual
kingdom, the universe, according to the Bible, has been
created to be the theatre, and in the interests of this
kingdom it is being governed. This is why of each
great constituent of the universe, and of the whole, it is
declared that it is "good", nay, "very good",—all is
fitted to minister to moral and spiritual ends. I do not
know that outside of, and apart from, the sphere of
Biblical influence this doctrine has ever been fully and
firmly grasped. In all ages a large proportion—perhaps

the vast majority—of the human race have regarded
Nature as being hostile to the moral and spiritual ; and
the material, as being the very seat and source of evil.
Even the Greek, with all his sense of Nature's beauty,
did not escape this pessimistic view of the universe.
But to the Biblical writers the material order is good,—
good as a whole, and good in all its parts. And yet
there is no pantheistic identification of Nature with God.
God remains distinct in His spiritual personality. Nor
is the conviction due to any defective sense of the reality
of evil. On the contrary the Biblical sense of evil is
intense. It is the same Psalmist who expresses the
purest joy in Nature and the most absolute contentment
with all Nature's ways, who also expresses the utmost
resentment against the " disproportioned sin " that

> " Jars against nature's chime, and with harsh din
>   Breaks the fair music that all creatures make
>   To their great Lord[1] ".

" Let sinners be consumed out of the earth, and let the
wicked be no more " (Ps. civ. 35).

We may thus sum up the Biblical interpretation of
the Self-manifestation of God in Nature :—Nature is the
immediate handiwork of the free, intelligent, sovereign
action of the personal God. This God must not be
identified with Nature, nor likened to any created thing :
He transcends Nature ; yet not in the sense of remote-
ness from it,—He is intimately close to it ; but in the
sense of sovereignly controlling it. Nature has been
created, and is being governed, for moral and spiritual
ends—the realisation of the kingdom of the good.

---

[1] Milton, *At a solemn Music* (with a change of tense).

Of the immense moral value of this view of the natural order there can be no doubt. Life, as we have seen, is an interaction between personality and environment. The conceptions we form of that environment immensely influence the colour and quality of life. We have seen the Biblical conception of our natural environment as being the handiwork of the perfectly good God, created and controlled by Him for ends of holy love. Now contrast with this the conception embodied in the following sonnet addressed to Nature:

> "Thou art not ' calm ', but restless as the ocean
> Filling with aimless toil the endless years—
> Stumbling on thought and throwing off the spheres,
> Churning the universe with mindless motion.
> Dull fount of joy, unhallow'd source of tears,
> Cold motor of our fervid faith and song,
> Dead, but engendering life, love, pangs, and fears,
> Thou crownedst thy wild work with foulest wrong,
> When first thou lightedst on a seeming goal
> And darkly blundered on man's suffering soul[1]".

Surely it must make an immense difference to our moral life according as we accept one or other of these pictures of our natural environment. The first must generate a courageous buoyancy of life; the second, a profound moral disheartenment. " It makes a tremendous emotional and practical difference to one", says Professor James, "whether one accepts the universe in the drab "discoloured way of Stoic resignation to necessity, or with "the passionate happiness of Christian saints. The dif-"ference is as great as that between passivity and activity, "as that between the defensive and aggressive mood "

---

[1] Emily Pfeiffer.

(*Varieties of Religious Experience*, p. 41).   The writer of
the sonnet from which I have quoted felt this :

> " Dead force, in whom of old we loved to see
> A nursing mother, clothing with her life
> The seeds of Love Divine, with what sore strife
> We hold or yield our thoughts of Love and Thee " !

Nor is the Biblical conception of the universe less
valuable from the scientific point of view.   The Bible
and science have often been placed in antagonism.   Yet
it is hardly an exaggeration to say that without the
Biblical conception, the progress of science would have
been well-nigh impossible.   It is not wholly an accident
that science has flourished most in Christendom.   For
one thing, man could make little progress in science
until he could feel confidence in Nature.   So long as he
dreaded it as something malignant, he dared not to
investigate its secrets.   It is, I believe, because the
Chinese regard Nature as bedevilled, that hitherto they
have failed to utilise the immense mineral resources of
their empire.   But the Biblical view, and the Biblical
view alone, inspires trust in Nature and casts out fear.
Then, too, the conception of Nature as the handiwork
of the One God, gives that idea of the unity of Nature
which is one of science's fundamental principles.   Again
the very idea of science involves the interpretability of
Nature ; for science is just the interpretation of Nature.
But that which is interpretable must be conceived as
being rational—the product of reason, and of reason
akin to man's.   Now the Bible gives us the very highest
conception of the rationality of the universe, by representing the universe as the expression of a wisdom not
less than Divine.   Thus in the Book of Proverbs, in a

splendid passage (ch. viii.), Wisdom is represented as presiding over the construction of the universe :

"When He established the heavens I (Wisdom) was there :
When He set a circle upon the face of the deep :
When He made firm the skies above :
When the fountains of the deep became strong :
When He gave to the sea its bound,
That the waters should not transgress His commandment :
When He marked out the foundations of the earth :
Then I (Wisdom) was by Him, as a master workman ".

And that this Divine Wisdom is akin to man's, follows from the fundamental principle of the Bible, that man is made in the image of God ; and, indeed, in the chapter of Proverbs from which I have quoted, the same Divine Wisdom that constructed the Universe, is represented as being also the Guide of man's life :

" By me kings reign,
And princes decree justice.
By me princes rule,
And nobles, even all the judges of the earth ".

Lastly the greatest impulse to scientific investigation in our time is the philanthropic impulse—the desire to make Nature minister to human well-being and advancement. And here too the Bible prepared the way by its doctrine that Nature has been created in subservience to the kingdom of God, which on its earthly side, is the kingdom of man :

"Thou madest him (man) scarce less than gods,
And didst crown him with honour and with state ;
And madest him to rule over the work of Thy hands,—
All things hast Thou put under his feet ".

(Ps. viii., Cheyne's translation.)

It is largely because the Bible, imperfectly known as it is, has, in the course of centuries, generated an atmosphere impregnated with these great ideas of Nature's trustworthiness, unity, rationality, subordination to human interests, that science has flourished within the sphere of Biblical influence, as it has not flourished where that influence has not penetrated[1].

The moral and scientific value of the Biblical conception of the universe, upon the criterion of truth adopted in these lectures, guarantees the validity of the conception ; and inspiration is an adequate account of the Biblical writer's success in attaining it.

[1] Cf. Gwatkin, *Knowledge of God*, vol. II. p. 273.

CHAPTER VII

BIBLICAL INTERPRETATION OF THE SELF-MANI-FESTATION OF GOD IN MAN'S MORAL CON-STITUTION

WE come now to the Biblical interpretation of God's Self-manifestation in man's moral constitution.

People of British descent, living in the twentieth century, ought not to need to have proved to them that the great outstanding feature of the prophets of Israel was their passion for righteousness, and that the litera-ture which they have bequeathed to us, is the world's great ethical classic. For British peoples Matthew Arnold has done that service once for all,—has done it with adequate knowledge of the world's great ethical teachers and their writings, with incomparable lucidity of expression and grace of style, and, what to the modern temper may seem more important, with the unconventionality and freedom of the layman.

Arnold found in the Biblical writers certain great qualities, which he did not find—not at least in anything like the same degree—in other ethical teachers. He found in them a high seriousness about morality. These men literally *felt* "conduct"—righteousness—to be a matter of life and death for men and nations. Righteous-ness was not merely one of the interests of life, which

must be content to take its chance among other interests
of equal, or even greater, importance,—it was *the* interest,
to which all others must be subordinated. He found,
too, an emotional glow in these men that was all their
own. He had found that ethical teaching, even when
true and noble and beautiful, is for the most part cold ;
and he knew that, however true and beautiful, a cold
ethic is impotent. He knew that men do wrong, not so
much from ignorance of the right and good, as from the
presence of evil feelings and passions ; and he knew that
these evil feelings and passions can only be conquered
by the awakening of higher feelings and passions[1]. Now,
he found that the Biblical writers had themselves this
ethical emotion in a supreme degree ; that it informed
their teachings ; and that those teachings, even on the
printed page, still glowed with it. And so he writes,
" As long as the world lasts, all who want to make
" progress in righteousness will come to Israel for in-
" spiration as to the people who have had the sense for
" righteousness strongest and most glowing ; and in
" hearing and reading the words Israel has uttered, those
" who care for conduct, will find a force and a stimulus
" they could find nowhere else. As well imagine a man
" with a sense for sculpture not cultivating it by the help
" of the remains of Greek art, or a man with a sense for
" poetry not cultivating it by the help of Homer and
" Dante, as a man with a sense for conduct not cultivating
" it by the help of the Bible. And this sense for conduct

---

[1] It is just here that we are to
find the weakness of the ethical
teaching of Socrates, the great Greek
teacher. Socrates identified virtue
with knowledge. He thought that
if men knew the right they would
do it. " He was apparently un-
"conscious of the power which the
"desires and the will of the ordi-
"nary man have to fight against his
"reason". (See Mill, *Apology of
Socrates*, p. 12.)

" is a sense which the generality of men have far more
" decidedly than they have the sense for art or for
" science. At any rate, whether this or that man has it
" decidedly or not, it is the sense which has to do with
" three-fourths of human life.

" This does constitute for Israel a most extraordinary
" distinction. In spite of all which in them and in their
" character is unattractive, nay, repellent,—in spite of
" shortcomings even in righteousness itself and their in-
" significance in everything else,—this petty, unsuccessful,
" unamiable people, without politics, without science,
" without art, without charm, deserve their great place
" in the world's regard, and are likely to have it more
" and more, as the world goes on, rather than less. It is
" secured to them by the facts of nature and by the
" unalterable constitution of things[1] ".

All this is most truly and admirably said. But when
Arnold comes to account for the intense and glowing
ethical feeling of the Biblical writers he is not so successful. He sets out in the right direction, but I venture to
think that he somewhat misses the goal. It will help us
to understand the matter, if we consider for a moment
man's moral constitution. There are two factors in man's
moral constitution that must be carefully distinguished.
There is, first, the faculty of moral judgement—the
faculty by which we decide, sometimes not without
painful deliberation, that this or that course of action is
right or wrong. Next, there is the authority, which,
with greater or less degree of strength and pressure,
obliges us to perform the action which we have judged
to be right. Now this faculty of judgement and this
authority are not identical. This is proved by the fact

[1] *Literature and Dogma*, pp. 42, 43.

that to decide that such and such an action is right, is not the same thing as to feel obligation to perform it. A man may have a delicate and exact faculty of moral discrimination and yet be lacking in any strong sense of moral obligation : moral distinctions are clearly perceived, the bindingness of them but feebly felt. On the other hand, a man's faculty of discrimination may be clumsy and blundering, while his sense of duty is imperious. This undoubted fact would seem to show that the authority in conscience is something different from the faculty of moral judgement. Now the faculty of moral judgement is undoubtedly ours : it is we who weigh and deliberate and at last decide that such and such a course is right. Is the authority also ours ? Do we merely order ourselves to follow the course we ourselves have judged to be right ? I cannot think so. I think it is something very like nonsense to speak of commanding ourselves, or of obeying or disobeying ourselves, or of being penitent and remorseful over our own self-disobedience. The authority indeed makes itself felt within us, but it is not *of* us ; its source is without us. In other words, there is that in our moral life that is not *we*. Now, Arnold perceived this fact, "the very great part in righteousness which belongs, we may say, to *not ourselves*". He believed that the Biblical writers perceived it more clearly than any other men ever did ; and he believed that it was their vivid percep-tion of this something *not themselves* in conscience that gave to their morality its emotional glow. In all this Arnold was profoundly right. Awe, reverence, love, cannot be felt towards that which is merely ourselves. But when Arnold proceeds to define what that some-thing not ourselves in conscience is, he seems woefully inadequate. He usually defines it by the adjective "eternal"—"the eternal"; but to this adjective he prefers not to supply a noun. Now an adjective, which is a qualifying term, without some thing or person that is qualified thereby, has no existence; nor does writing it with a capital E make it any the more real. Certainly an adjective cannot evoke any strong or deep emotion; it is like a blank cheque, valueless until it is filled up. We want to know what or who is eternal, before we can be strongly affected by, or towards, it. Arnold does, indeed, at times supply a noun. The Eternal *not ourselves* is "the stream of tendency by which all things seek to fulfil the law of their being". But it is safe to say that a "stream of tendency" is quite incapable of evoking the ethical ardour Arnold so justly extols in the Biblical writers. The fact is, feelings of solemn, reverential, adoring love can only be evoked by what is personal. This statement may be thought to be too sweeping. It may be thought that such feelings are often called forth by the contemplation of Nature. This is true, but it is to be observed that when we are thus affected towards Nature, it is because we have, for the moment, personified her. This is proved by the fact that in such moments we apply epithets to Nature which denote personal attributes, speaking of her as "wise", "kind", "bountiful", "prodigal", etc. These are the attributes of persons and would be unmeaning upon the lips of one for whom

> "Earth goes by chemic forces; Heaven's
> A Mécanique Céleste"!

No; reverential, loving, admiring emotion can only be evoked by that which is conceived, and strongly conceived, as personal,—as thinking, feeling, willing, being.

And beyond all doubt such was the view of the Biblical writers. Read Ps. cxxxix., probably the grandest hymn ever addressed to the something not ourselves in the moral life, "which", as Arnold says, "weighed upon the mind of Israel and engaged its awe", and ask yourselves whether that marvellous intermingling of trembling awe, longing, gratitude, adoration, praise, could ever have been poured forth to an adjective, or even to a stream of tendency. That Psalm indeed shows us with what emotional ardours the Old Testament ethical life glowed; but it also shows that the source of the emotion was the profound realisation of the fact that the pressure upon the conscience, the authority not to be gainsaid within, was the pressure of a living Will.

Arnold, indeed, admits that "Israel personified his "Eternal, for he was strongly moved, he was an orator "and a poet". But he goes on to say that "Israel did "not scientifically predicate *personality* of God; he would "not even have had a notion what was meant by it". The latter part of this statement we shall consider presently; of the former part, it may be enough to say that it presents a strange inversion of the true order of cause and effect. "Israel", he says, "personified his Eternal because he was strongly moved". The process was indubitably the reverse; he was strongly moved because he recognised his Eternal as personal. Had it occurred to him that the Eternal was *not* personal, his ethical nature would have remained cold.

Now, why did Arnold give this paradoxical account of the Old Testament conception of the authority confessed by conscience? Well; in the first place, he seems to have been misled by an erroneous explanation of the Divine name JEHOVAH. He seems to have thought that

"Eternal" was the exact English equivalent of this name. But the best Hebraists of our time reject this interpretation as philologically untenable. The God whom the Hebrews designated JEHOVAH is indeed eternal; but His eternity is not denoted by this name[1]. But Arnold was probably even more misled by a consideration, most true and important in itself, but from which he drew a strangely erroneous inference. He rightly perceived that the ancient Hebrew mind was unspeculative and unmetaphysical in its bent. From this he argues that the Hebrew mind could not have predicated personality of God, and would not even have had a notion what was meant by personality: for personality is a metaphysical conception. As Professor Momerie has pointed out, Arnold, in his reasoning, is confusing the perception of metaphysical facts[2] with the capacity for metaphysical reasoning. One may be quite capable of apprehending a metaphysical fact, without being able to reason about it or even knowing the meaning of the word metaphysical; just as one may be quite capable of perceiving physical facts without being able to reason about them or even knowing the meaning of the word physical. The ancient Hebrew certainly could not have reasoned about personality as a Hegel or a Kant might reason; but he was just as fully aware that he himself was a being who thought and felt and willed, as any philosopher could be, and there was no reason in the world why he should not believe that the Power, Who ruled his life,

[1] For the true meaning of JE-HOVAH in the historical religion of Israel, see ch. VIII.

[2] By a metaphysical fact is meant a fact not of the physical or phenomenal order, but of the spiritual and real order,—a fact belonging to the realm of ultimate reality and of causes, which underlies the physical and phenomenal. Personality is such a metaphysical fact. Cf. Momerie, *Inspiration and Other Sermons*, p. 68.

thought and willed, too. He would probably not have understood you if you had spoken to him about the "personality" of God, but he would have understood you just as little if you had spoken about his own "personality". But he knew quite well that he himself thought and felt and willed, and had no difficulty whatever in believing that God could do the same. Indeed his unspeculative bent made it easier for him thus to think ; for thus to think of the Power or Powers in the universe with which we have to do, is the first instinctive impulse of our nature ; and it is precisely the intrusion of metaphysical speculation that weakens this impulse. It was the Hebrew's inability to indulge in such specula-tion, that enabled him to give to the world the warm and vivid conception of God as personal that he has given. Moreover, it is strange that Arnold did not perceive that he was crediting the Hebrew with an exceptionally high degree of speculative faculty, when he represented him as being profoundly moved by the difficult conception of eternalness, dissociated from any concrete being whose quality it is.

But the chief cause of Arnold's misreading of Old Testament ways of thinking, is probably to be found in his exaggerated dislike of anthropomorphism. Arnold's contempt for those whose God was a "non-natural, magnified man" was unbounded. Yet anthropomorphism of some kind is inevitable. We are men and cannot help thinking the thoughts of men and speaking the language of men. Arnold himself does not hesitate to speak of the *not ourselves* as Power ; but power is quite as anthropomorphic a conception as personality : it is a conception derived from our human consciousness of will. All that those who speak of the Ultimate Reality

as Power or Force[1] do is to substitute a lower anthropomorphic conception for a higher; for we cannot help
regarding personality as the highest form of being that
we know. And it is sheer perversity to maintain that
the source from which personality comes is lower in the
scale of being than its offspring. The Divine Nature must
at least *include* personality. If instead of caricaturing
the Christian doctrine of the Holy Trinity, Arnold had
sympathetically studied it, he would perhaps have seen
that one of the chief values of that doctrine is, that it
safeguards us against excessive anthropomorphism of the
"non-natural, magnified man" type. For the doctrine
of the Holy Trinity means that while the Divine Nature
includes personality, it is also supra-personal[2].

I have criticised Arnold's position at some length,
because I feel strongly that the confusions into which
he has fallen, must largely neutralise the immense service
he has rendered by pointing out the unique value of the
Biblical ethical teaching, and by tracing that value to
its true source in the clearness with which the Biblical
writers perceived, and the intensity of emotion with
which they felt, an Authority in man's moral constitution, which man did not set up and which he cannot
dethrone. To the Hebrew the voice which says "thou

[1] "We must emphasise this—that "the idea of God as mere power is "simply unmeaning. It is not even "untrue but simply unmeaning. "Power without will to set it in "motion is potential, not active "power such as we see. It is like "the power stored in a piece of coal, "which can do nothing till it is put "on the fire. God as mere power is "a subject without a predicate, and "though we may sympathise with a "lament that the predicate cannot be "found, it is hard to understand "that the sentence can be all the "better for having no predicate"— Gwatkin, *Knowledge of God*, vol. I. pp. 83, 84.

[2] Existence in tri-personal unity, whatever else it is, is certainly not a human mode of being. Those who wish to see the bearing of the doctrine of the Holy Trinity upon the question of the personality of God, are referred to D'Arcy's *Idealism and Theology*.

oughtest" is none other than the Voice of the Righteous
Lord Who loveth righteousness, the pressure of obligation upon his will, none other than the pressure of the
Ultimate and Absolute Will. The ethical life was to
him "essentially a dialogue[1]". The cause of goodness,
justice and truth revealed itself to him and in him as
the Will of Another,—yet not of a stranger, but of his
"Great Companion", the Shepherd of his soul, guiding
him with his eye, leading him in paths of righteousness.
And so it appealed not to his conscience and will only,
but to his affections also—

> "Oh how love I thy law!
>   It is my meditation all the day.
>   How sweet are thy words unto my taste!
>   Yea, sweeter than honey to my mouth"!

And it was the unmetaphysical bent of his mind that
enabled him to feel this. He did not weaken and
confuse his first fresh intuition by ingenious speculations
regarding the "seat of authority" in morals,—speculations which, as we well know, too often rather explain
away than explain aright man's sense of obligation.

This Hebrew conception of a duality in the moral
life,—of morality as a thing in which man has to do with
God,—is seen in the Hebrew conception of righteousness. As far as the character of the righteous man is
concerned, the highest Old Testament ideal is largely
identical with our own. Both the Old Testament and
we would agree in regarding as righteous the character
delineated in the Fifteenth Psalm or in Job xxxi. 5 ff.
But there is a difference. The possession of that character,
according to our view, in itself constitutes righteous-

---

[1] See Tyrrell, *Lex Credendi*, p. 178.

ness, and we enquire no further. But for the Hebrew, possession of the character does not in itself constitute righteousness. Righteousness is with him predominantly a forensic term—a term of the law-court. The righteous man is properly the justified man—the man who has been pronounced in the right by the judge[1]. To be righteous, then, meant for the Hebrew to be right before God the Judge of all the earth ; and the man who is in this happy position is the man whose ethical character is what we call righteous. This I cannot but think is a far richer conception than ours, a conception of far greater moral dynamic. When we think of righteousness we have merely a certain type of character before our minds ; when the Hebrew thought of righteousness he, too, had that type of character in view ; but he had more,—he had also in view the judgement-seat of God, and man standing thereat and awaiting sentence. It is the absence of this tremendous conception from our modern secular systems of ethics that renders those systems so flat and impotent.

But to all this it may be said, " We admit that the " Hebrew way of looking at things does indeed supply a "strong emotional reinforcement to morality; nevertheless " does it not logically make God responsible for our errors " of moral judgement ? You say that God, speaking in " conscience, directly bids us do what, in any given case, " we have judged to be right. But we are not infallible, " we may, and sometimes do, decide wrongly. Does God " then bid us do what, however right it may seem to us, " is really wrong"? It must be admitted that some

---

[1] Of this predominantly forensic conception of righteousness we have curious evidence in the fact that the feminine form of the Hebrew adjective *righteous* never occurs. The affairs of men alone came before the courts. See Davidson, *Theology of the Old Testament*, p. 268.

such conclusion as this does follow from the Hebrew view. But three things may be said : (1) The obligation to do what we have judged to be right obviously involves the obligation to use all means of arriving at a right judgement. Now he who sincerely believes that the former obligation is the direct pressure upon his will of the Divine Will, will believe that the latter is so too, and will have the greatest possible incentive to use all means to arrive at a right decision,—an incentive more potent far than any he can have who traces the general sense of obligation to some lower source. (2) Such effort on our part is absolutely necessary if we are ever to attain moral manhood. If in addition to that pressure of His Will which urges us to do the right, God also, on each occasion, infallibly told us what is right, we should remain throughout life mere children in morality. It is better that, upon occasion, we should innocently err, than that we should never become "full-grown men, "even those who by reason of use have their senses exer-"cised to discern good and evil" (Heb. v. 14). (3) It is in the nature of things impossible for us to believe that God could ever command us to do wrong, or other than to do right. But it is equally impossible in the nature of things for us to distinguish what *seems* to us to be right from what objectively is right; as well try to run away from ourselves. What seems to us to be right, for all practical purposes, *is* right ; what seems to us to be wrong, for all practical purposes, *is* wrong. If then God is to be conceived as interested in our moral life at all, we must think of Him as bidding us do what we believe to be right. Further, since what seems to us to be right is by us indistinguishable from what is really right, if we refuse to do it, we as plainly show that we are persons who prefer something else above right, as if we had refused to obey a precept written by the finger of God across the sky. But what God desires is the production, not of a faultless machine warranted to produce the requisite number of objectively right acts *per diem*, but a character steadfastly set upon righteousness, unallured by pleasure and unaffrighted by pain. For, as Kant says, " Nothing can possibly be " conceived in the world or even out of it, which can be " called good except a Good Will[1]".

Such then being the character of the Old Testament ethics, it is passing strange that to not a few people the Old Testament seems to be known chiefly as a book which presents grave moral difficulties,—a book in which many things are recorded,—sometimes without a word of censure, sometimes with apparent approval—which shock the modern conscience. And these " moral difficulties" constitute for many minds the chief stumbling-block to belief in any real inspiration. What is to be said? Well; for one thing, we must remember that, even if no mitigation of these difficulties were forthcoming, they cannot obliterate those characteristics of the Old Testament upon which Matthew Arnold laid such stress, and which he illustrates by such copious quotation. If it be true that the Book of Genesis passes no censure upon the falsities of Jacob, this in no wise robs of its ethical power the doctrine of the Book of Proverbs, " Lying lips are an abomination to the LORD " (Prov. xii. 22). We should simply have to admit that, from the ethical point of view, the Old Testament is a collection of books of very unequal value. This might be true, and yet it might also be true that its most

[1] *Metaphysic of Ethics*, p. 10 (Abbott's translation).

valuable parts were so valuable as to constitute the collection, as a whole, the most potent instrument after the New Testament of moral education that the world possesses. Such a view, indeed, would be inconsistent with the theory of verbal inspiration; but that theory we have seen reason to reject on other grounds (ch. III.).

But there is something to be said in mitigation of the moral difficulties in question. (1) We have seen that four-fifths of the Old Testament is history. Now it is not the wont of historians to pause at every base and foul deed they record to express their personal disapproval of it; nor are we wont to suspect them of secretly approving, unless they do this. The historian assumes that his readers will credit him with the usual sentiments of upright men. And there are two reasons which render such reticence on the part of the Biblical historians especially natural. (*a*) Among the ancient Hebrews there was a strong dramatic element. For whatever reason, this element did not lead to the creation of a distinct literature of the Drama, such, e.g., as ancient Greece developed. But what it lacked of concentration it gained of diffusion. The dramatic element permeated the whole national literature, to a greater extent probably than can be paralleled elsewhere. Hebrew lyric poetry and prophetic oratory are both highly dramatic. And the same characteristic marks Hebrew history-writing[1]. Now it is of the essence of dramatic writing that the author does not appear. He presents to us personages, their words and actions and circumstances, and also the

---

[1] " If such things could be made " the subject of measurement, it " would be safe to predict that the " *mass* of dramatic material in " Biblical literature would not be " less than that found in other litera- " tures where Drama is a distinct " form ". Professor Moulton, *Literary Study of the Bible*, p. 111.

sequence of events; but he himself keeps in the back-
ground, nor obtrudes upon us his own comments. In
writing of this kind it is absurd to suppose that the
author approves of everything that everybody says and
does. No one dreams that Shakspere approved of
treachery and murder because he does not tell us in an
"aside" that in his private opinion Macbeth is a villain.
(*b*) In the view of the Hebrew historians, history itself
was a drama (see ch. VIII.), in which God is the chief
Personage. It is what God thinks of men and their
actions that the historian is most anxious to show us;
and what God thinks is seen in the slow working-out of
consequences. One who holds this view of history
becomes an awe-struck spectator, and to interject his
own verdict would be in his view a profane impertinence.
Apply this to the case of Jacob. It is true that the
historian expresses no personal judgement upon that
miserable story of feminine ambition, parental partiality,
deception, meanness, selfishness, falsity. But he lets us
see what the scheming mother and too-willing son got
by their plotting. Rebecca gained by it final separation
from her son; she never saw Jacob again. It gained
Jacob terrified flight from his father's roof; twenty years
of exile; dread of his brother's wrath, which at the end
of twenty years still haunted him. It made him the
victim in Laban's service of a multiplied deceit similar
to his own. Treachery and unbrotherliness in his own
household well-nigh brought his gray hairs in sorrow to
the grave. At last in old age, casting up "life's chequered
sum", he is forced to confess that few and evil have been
the days of his pilgrimage. Perhaps we think that if
they were evil, it was well that they were few; but that
is not Jacob's thought,—they were few and yet they were

all unhappy. I hold that this impersonal, silent presentation of the unerring, inevitable judgement of God is infinitely more impressive than any moralisings of the historian could possibly be. It awes us ; it subdues us ; it forces us to realise that over us there is an "infinite rigour of law", even if there be "infinite pity", too. But it may be said, "Nevertheless the Book of Genesis "represents Jacob as the chosen of God, while Esau, so "much more amiable, it represents as rejected". This is true. But we must remember that Esau, with all his attractive qualities, had one absolutely fatal defect : he was incapable of subordinating the present to the future, —of foregoing an immediate gratification for the sake of a distant good. Now Jacob, with all his grievous faults, had this power of far-sighted self-control. This power may not be in itself a virtue ; but it is the *conditio sine qua non* of any solid and enduring virtue. The man who has it can be made something of; he may need stern treatment,—Jacob needed such treatment, and the Divine choice did not exempt him from it,—but he will profit by it. Whereas, the other type of man is that fool from whom, though he be brayed in a mortar, his folly will not depart. Your quarrel over the preference shown to Jacob is not with the Book of Genesis but with *Life*; for it is only to the man who can live for the future that *Life* gives a future.

(2) Among the things that shock us, especially in the earlier Hebrew history, is the barbarity with which the Jew treated his enemies. In this he was no whit worse than other ancient peoples, possibly a trifle better. Nevertheless his standard was not that which Christ has taught us to observe. Now we must remember that for whatever reason, the moral education of the race, like all

other education, has been gradual. But a system of gradual education means that some truths are learned later than others. Now if man has indeed a Divine Educator, it will not be a matter of chance which lessons are taught first, and which are postponed to a later stage. There will be wise reasons for the order observed. It would be a stupendous task to attempt to discover these reasons in the varied moral education of all the peoples of the world. But perhaps it may not be impossible to suggest a reason in the case of the Hebrew people. The Hebrews have given ethical monotheistic religion to the world. Theists must believe that this was the task assigned them as a people by God (see ch. IX.). Their course of education, then, would be shaped with a view to this task. Now, for centuries they were the sole monotheistic people in the midst of a polytheistic world. They were, too, a small and insignificant people. History tells us, what indeed we should expect, that they were in continual danger of yielding to the potent heathen influences that surrounded them. In such circumstances, their safety, the safety of the Divine treasure entrusted to them, lay in the inculcation of a stern exclusiveness. Had the lesson of a wide humanity—of brotherliness towards all men—been the lesson emphasised at that stage, it would practically have meant a brotherliness in religion as well as in other things, and ethical monotheism, which was destined to be, and which alone can be, the foundation of a world-wide humanity, would have perished. But though the lesson of humanity was postponed, it was not forgotten. The germ of it was already present in the Old Testament doctrine of the unity of the human race as sprung from a single pair ; and in the fulness of time to this fiercely exclusive people, and through them to the world, was given, by precept and example, the truth of the brotherhood of man, which even to-day the world rather admires than practises. Further, if we believe that it was not a matter of chance among what people the Christian Ethic should arise, and to whom it should be first proclaimed, then we must further believe that the Israel of the first century A.D. was the one people best fitted to serve as a centre and starting-point for Christianity, and this in itself justifies the method of Israel's education in the preceding ages.

(3)   It follows from the principle of gradual education in morals, that in judging the moral standard in any given age, we ought to compare it with the standards that have preceded it, not with those that have followed it.   A standard which may be relatively low when compared with one that has superseded it, may be relatively high when compared with one that preceded it.   Accordingly, the question regarding any given standard of morals is not, Does it fully embody the moral ideal? but, Is it such an advance upon preceding standards as to show that the people whose standard it is, have their faces set towards the ideal?   Thus, from the standpoint of the Christian Moral Ideal, the Mosaic *lex talionis*— "An eye for an eye, and a tooth for a tooth"—is woefully defective; Christianity shows a more excellent way. But compared with the practice of unlimited revenge which preceded it, perpetuating blood-feuds from father to son, it marks an amazing ethical advance.   As it occurs in the Mosaic legislation, it does not so much express approval as impose restriction—"You must not "demand more than an eye for an eye, or a tooth for "a tooth".   Again, slavery is the very negation of all that Christianity has taught us as to the intrinsic worth

of man as man, yet in its origin it was a great improvement upon the wholesale massacre of prisoners of war which it superseded[1]; and in the restricted form in which it is permitted in the Mosaic legislation, marks a distinct advance in humanity. The question of Divorce is especially instructive as to the different moral value a standard will have according as it is compared with that which preceded it or with that which follows. The Mosaic law permits divorce under certain legal restrictions and after certain legal formalities have been complied with (Deut. xxiv. 1–4)[2]. Modern States also permit divorce, with certain legal restrictions and formalities. Are then the Mosaic law and the latest colonial Divorce Act of the same ethical quality? By no means. It is hardly an exaggeration to say that they are of opposite ethical quality. They seem to be at the same point; but it is as persons, who are travelling in opposite directions, for the moment meet. The Mosaic law is essentially restrictive; it seeks to supersede an earlier custom of arbitrary divorce, which permitted the *man* to put away his partner at will, and without reason assigned. The modern law is laxative; it removes restrictions formerly imposed. The Mosaic law has its face set towards the ideal of the strictly monogamic family; the modern law, alas! has turned its back upon that ideal[3].

---

[1] "Hence the Justinian Code and "also St Augustine (*De Civ. Dei*, "XIX. 15) derived servus from "'servare', to preserve, because the "victor preserved his prisoners "alive".—Lecky, *History of European Morals*, vol. I. p. 102.

[2] "The rendering of A.V., R.V., "is not here quite exact; v. 1–3 form "the protasis, stating the conditions "of the case contemplated, v. 4 is the "apodosis".—*International Critical Commentary on Deuteronomy*, p. 269.

[3] Those who think that the modern tendency to facilitate divorce is a sign of enlightenment and progress would do well to remember that it is in reality a reversion to an earlier condition of things. The strictly

I think that the considerations here suggested—the strongly dramatic character of Hebrew history-writing and the gradualness of moral education—will, if carefully weighed, to some extent at least, mitigate the moral difficulties of the Old Testament.

(4) But there is one class of difficulties with which I wish to deal somewhat more fully, since it is one that specially forces itself upon the attention of English Church people. I mean the so-called Imprecatory Psalms, which are sung or said in our churches in their due order in the Psalter. It is not, however, of the use of these psalms in our worship that I wish to speak, but of their place in the Old Testament. I believe that on this point we may derive much aid from modern criticism.

More than forty years ago Professor Seeley in *Ecce Homo* had made suggestions which gave welcome relief to many minds. He pointed out[1] that in the history of the treatment of crime there had been three stages: the stage of barbarous insensibility, the stage of law or justice, and that of humanity. The first stage, that of moral insensibility, he finds represented in the *Iliad* of Homer. " In that poem the distinction between right "and wrong is barely recognised; and the distinction " of mankind into the good and the bad is not recognised " at all. It has often been remarked that it contains no "villain. The reason of this is not that the poet does "not represent his characters as doing wicked deeds, for, "in fact, there is not one among them that is not capable

monogamic family is the outcome of a long upward struggle of humanity, taught by experience that monogamy is essential to a staple and effective social life. The provision by modern States of facilities of divorce and remarriage is the virtual abandonment of the ideal of the monogamic family, and the introduction into their life of a principle already proved to be fatal to stability and effectiveness. Cf. Professor Peabody, *Jesus Christ and the Social Question*, pp. 137 ff.

[1] *Ecce Homo*, pp. 233 ff.

"of deeds the most atrocious and shameful. But the
"poet does not regard these deeds with any strong dis-
"approbation, and the feeling of moral indignation which
"has been so strong in later poets is in him so feeble
"that he is quite incapable of hating any of his characters
"for their crimes. He can no more conceive the notion
"of a villain than of an habitually virtuous man. The
"few deeds that he recognises as wrong or at least as
"strange and dangerous,—killing a suppliant, or killing
"a father—he, notwithstanding, conceives all persons
"alike as capable of perpetrating under the influence
"of passion or some heaven-sent bewilderment of the
"understanding". Such is the stage of moral insensibility. There is no consciousness of wrong-doing as the
violation of a moral order. Wrong-doing is simply an
affront or a damage to the person injured by it, which
the onlooker views with complete indifference.

The next stage came probably with the advent of
written law, when a sense of justice began to diffuse
itself through the community. With written law "a
"fixed standard of action is set up which serves to each
"man as a rule of life for himself and a rule of criticism
"upon his neighbours. Then comes the division of
"mankind into those who habitually conform to this rule
"and those who violate it, into the good and the bad,
"and feelings soon spring up to sanction the classification,
"feelings of respect for the one class and hatred for the
"other". Men do not any longer view with indifference
an act of wrong done to another. With the injured
they sympathise, but for the injurer they have no
sympathy, simply resentment and hatred.

The third and highest stage is the stage of mercy or
humanity, which Seeley defines as "pity and disappro-

bation or resentment mixed ". In this stage, of which the Life and teaching of Christ is the supreme illustration, hatred of wrong as wrong and sympathy with the injured remain undiminished. But a new element has entered in, viz., a sense of the essential misery of sin even when it flourishes like a green bay-tree, and so, while wrong is hated and sympathy is felt with its victim, pity is felt for the wrong-doer, and a new thing appears, viz., mercy, in which indignation and pity are mixed. So long indeed as the wrong-doer is insolent and triumphant, the pity of the merciful man will be held in abeyance, and indignation alone given scope. But when the wrong-doer has been brought low, when he has paid his penalty, the merciful man does not dismiss the matter from his thoughts. He considers that the criminal also has claims upon him, claims so strong that they are not forfeited by any atrocity of crime. Such, according to Professor Seeley, have been the three steps in the treatment of crime. As he finds the first stage represented in the Homeric poems, and the third represented in the Christian Gospels, so he finds the second represented in the Psalter. The moral development of the Hebrews advanced more rapidly than that of the heathen peoples ; and while the latter were still oscillating between the stage of moral insensibility and the stage of hatred towards wickedness, the Hebrews had definitely entered upon the latter stage. The division between the good and the bad was more sharply and deeply drawn among them than elsewhere, and the vindictive Psalms remain to tell us how unmixed the hatred of the bad was.

Such is Seeley's view, and it gave immense relief. It at once justified the presence of the vindictive Psalms in a book which, in one aspect of it, is the record of the moral education of mankind.

I have no doubt that Seeley has rightly sketched for us the course that human education has historically taken; and it may well be that traces of that education are to be found in a book so many-sided and so human as the Hebrew Psalter. Nevertheless his account of the vindictive Psalms, however true it may be of some of them, is not quite that which criticism gives of those Psalms as a whole.

Criticism does two things for these Psalms: (*a*) it reveals their true character; (*b*) it gives them their true historical setting.

(*a*) According to criticism, these Psalms, as a whole, are not the individual and personal utterances they have been supposed to be. The speaker in them is not speaking as an individual, bemoaning his private and personal sorrows and wrongs, nor are the evil-doers denounced members of the criminal class in the ordinary sense, committing acts of aggression upon the life, the property, the honour of their fellow-citizens,—the people who in these days frequent our gaols. The speaker bears a representative character; he is the spokesman of a group; the " I ", the " my ", the " me " of these Psalms is collective not individual[1]. This group may be the whole nation of Israel, or it may be the pious kernel— the church, not as a mere human organisation, but as representing, and conscious of representing, a Cause— the Cause of JEHOVAH, of the true religion, in the world. A time came in the history of Israel's religion when that religion " from being naïve, and instinctive and "unconscious in its utterances and life, attained to

[1] For further remarks upon this point, see ch. IX.

" reflection on itself and the consciousness of its own
" meaning. The conflict of the nation with other nations
" and their mixture among the peoples of the world
" gave the people a knowledge of the world religions,
" and compelled comparison with their own. And their
" own was true, the others false[1]". And religion meant
for them not a set of opinions, but the realisation of
the kingdom of God in the world (see ch. IX.). The
establishment of this kingdom is the *dénouement* of the
historic movement; and meantime the cause of the
kingdom is entrusted to Israel. Such being the speaker
in these Psalms, the enemies denounced are not personal
enemies, not ordinary criminals ; they are insolent and
aggressive foes of the true religion, of the cause of the
kingdom of God,—sometimes domestic enemies within
Israel, like the persecutors of Jeremiah and his disciples,
or like the paganising party in the Maccabean period ;
sometimes, and more often, some aggressive heathen
nation or ruler. Accordingly it is not personal resentment or malice that breathes in these Psalms,—not at
all the feeling that flames up in our breasts when some
one has injured us, and that prompts us to pay him
back in his own coin—with liberal interest added. It is
the Cause of God—which means the cause of humanity—
that is at stake, and the flame that burns is the flame
of righteous indignation against the enemies of God
and man. And here we find the explanation of another
feature of these Psalms that has given great offence, viz.,
the apparent self-righteousness of the speakers. They
seem to plead their own righteousness, and to assert
their own righteousness, before God with a boldness that
shocks those who realise how imperfect human nature

[1] Davidson, *Theology of the Old Testament*, p. 137.

is, even at its best. But, as a matter of fact, the speakers are not thinking of their own personal characters at all. We have here an instance of the "forensic" use of the term righteousness, to which I have already drawn attention. Righteousness in this connexion means not ethical character, but *right cause*. When they plead before God that they are righteous as against assailing foes, they mean, not that they are morally faultless, but that they are in the right, that their cause—the cause of God Himself—is righteous, and that they are calling upon God not to vindicate their integrity, but His own cause which He has committed into their hands[1]. A man might feel and speak thus—feel and speak strongly—and yet be very lowly in his own eyes.

(*b*) All this becomes clearer if we consider the historical situations to which criticism assigns the vindictive Psalms. These situations are four: (1) The persecution of Jeremiah and his associates by those who are pushing the national religion to destruction. (2) The brutal cruelty of Edom and Moab at the time of the destruction of Jerusalem by the Babylonians. (3) The treachery of Sanballat and Tobiah (Neh. ii.—vi.), which threatened the very life of the community of the Restoration. (4) The persecutions of Antiochus Epiphanes which aimed at nothing less than the extermination of the worshippers of JEHOVAH. To this last period the majority of the imprecations belong. Such are the historical situations assigned by Criticism to the vindictive Psalms. It is exceedingly difficult for us to realise how critical, at least to human view, these situations were for the Divine cause and the hope of the world. Happily,

---

[1] Davidson, *Theology of the Old Testament*, p. 138.

in our time that cause and that hope are no longer bound
up with the fortunes of one weak and insignificant people,
nay, with a small fragment of such a people. That cause
and that hope have now their citadels stationed in every
land under heaven, and their watchwords are spoken in
more than two hundred tongues. To-day Christendom
might perish, but the Church of God would remain. But
it was otherwise in the days of our Psalmists. One
feeble people—at times one small section of a people—
had the human guardianship of the destinies of mankind;
and not once nor twice the guardian seemed about to
perish at the hands of ruthless foes. In such circumstances we can understand the passionate pleadings of
the people of God:—

> "Yea, for Thy sake are we killed all the day long;
> We are counted as sheep for the slaughter.
> Awake, why sleepest Thou, O Lord?
> Arise, cast us not off for ever.
> Wherefore hidest Thou Thy face,
> And forgettest our affliction and our oppression"?
>
> > (Ps. xliv. 22–24.)
>
> "Arise, O God, plead Thine own cause:
> Remember how the impudent[1] man reproacheth Thee all
> the day.
> Forget not the voice of Thine adversaries,
> The tumult of those that rise up against Thee ascendeth
> continually". (Ps. lxxiv. 22, 23).

Such then is the account which criticism gives of the
imprecations in the Psalter. But what are we to say of
the spirit that they breathe? Are we simply to say that
it was excusable in the historical situation, but that it is
not admirable, is not Christian? There are, I think, few

---

[1] "Foolish" of A.V., R.V. in-
correct; see *International Critical*
Commentary on Psalms, vol. i.
p. 109.

matters in which we Christians more err from the spirit
of Christ than in the matter of resentment and indignation.   And we err in two directions.   Christians though
we are, we do not mind cherishing and uttering bitter
feelings against those who have done us, it may be, some
trifling injury; and this Christ both by word and example
has absolutely forbidden: on the cross He prayed for
His enemies.   But we think the spirit of the vindictive
Psalms utterly reprehensible; yet Christ Himself exemplified it.   In all the vindictive Psalms there is nothing
more vehement than Christ's denunciation of the enemies
of the Kingdom of God in His own day (Matt. xxiii.).
The spirit of the vindictive Psalms is not alien from the
Christian spirit; it is an essential element of it[1].   What
is alien from the Christian spirit is the decadent "lenient
moralism" so characteristic of this age, and so compatible
with much personal spite and malice.   We should be
vastly more Christian if the forces of personal resentment
burned less fiercely within us, while the fires of righteous
indignation against the enemies of God and man glowed
with intenser flame.   What does mark these Psalms as
belonging to an ethical stage less advanced than
Christianity, is not their spirit of indignant antagonism,
but the form in which it clothes itself, especially the
physical sufferings imprecated not only upon the actual
foes but upon their wives, their children, even the unborn.
This last feature is due to the ancient conception of an
unqualified solidarity of life, according to which the
whole social group was held responsible for the sins of its
members.   Solidarity, as we shall see (ch. X.), is a great
fact and a great factor in human life; but we have learned,

[1] The spirit of Milton's sonnet, "Avenge, O Lord, thy slaughtered saints" is not more Hebraic than Christian.

chiefly through Christian teaching, that there exists side by side with it a sacred reserve of individuality. The innocent may inevitably suffer with the guilty, but they must not be punished as guilty[1].

Such then are the considerations that may be urged in mitigation of the moral difficulties of the Old Testament. Probably they will appeal with varying cogency to different minds. But, as I have already remarked, these difficulties, relieved or unrelieved, cannot obliterate those characteristics which make the Old Testament the world's great ethical classic,—the seriousness and ardour of its ethical enthusiasm, born of the simplicity, the directness, the strength, with which it realises that righteousness has its seat in the bosom of a Personal Will, Whose contact creates man's sense of obligation, and in Whose favour is life. And if these difficulties still puzzle us, then let us remember that it is from the Old Testament we have got that very conception of God as a Righteous Being and of the bindingness of righteousness, without which we should not feel them to be difficulties at all. (See the *Life of F. D. Maurice*, vol. I. p. 517.)

[1] Upon the whole question of the imprecations in the Psalter see *International Critical Commentary*, vol. I. pp. xcix, c, to which I am much indebted.

CHAPTER VIII

BIBLICAL INTERPRETATION OF THE SELF-MANIFESTATION OF GOD IN HISTORY

WE have now come to that which was the chief interest of the Biblical writers,—the interpretation of history. It has been truly said that for ancient Israel "History had a deeper significance than it had for any "other people....It was...the source from which they "drew ethical and spiritual enlightenment. Thither they "turned as to living oracles inscribed with the fingers of "the Almighty[1]". I have already pointed out (ch. III.) that four-fifths of the Old Testament is concerned with history. Now this emphasis upon history is not accidental. We have seen (ch. IV.) that character, human or Divine, can only be adequately revealed in *acts*. Deeds, not words alone, reveal moral quality. But a further element is needed for a full revelation of character, the element of time. Power, indeed, may be displayed in a single mighty deed; but not faithfulness, justice, love. For the display óf these, time is needed. The false man, the unjust man, the selfish man, may, once in a way, do acts that are materially true, just, loving ; but

---

[1] A comparison of the Psalter with any modern hymn-book will show the profound religious meaning history had for Israel.

to show that the man himself is true, just, loving, requires prolonged and consistent courses of action in many different situations and circumstances. It is not otherwise with God. For His full Self-manifestation time is needed. "His power He could reveal in one terrible "act, but the principles lying behind His power and "governing the exercise of it,—His justice, His goodness, "His grace, in a word His moral nature,—could not be "shown except by a prolonged exhibition of Himself "in relation to the life of man" (Davidson, *Theology of the Old Testament*, p. 7). Hence the Old Testament emphasis upon history. We have there the record of a section of human history, and an interpretation thereof, covering something like a thousand years. True, it is chiefly the history of a single people, Israel; yet not of Israel in isolation, but of Israel as, during a thousand years, it came into varying contact with the great peoples of the world, Egypt, Assyria, Babylonia, Persia, Greece. Of this great history we have both narrative and interpretation. The narrative is given chiefly in the historical books; the interpretation, chiefly, in the prophetical books; but in both respects these writings overlap. It is one of the greatest boons of Criticism that it has rescued the prophetic writings out of the hands of prediction-mongers, and shown the Prophets as interpreters of their own age, enabling us, for the most part, definitely to assign them their place in history. Each Prophet stands in closest connexion with some crisis in the history; claims to possess an insight into its meaning; to understand its purpose, and to discern its end. Thus, to take a few examples, Isaiah (740–700 B.C.) is associated with two crises, the Syro-Ephraimitish War and the Assyrian Invasion; Jeremiah (626–586 B.C.), with

the decline and fall of the Jewish State before Nebu-·
chadnezzar; Ezekiel (592–570 B.C.), with the Babylonian
Exile; II. Isaiah (540 B.C.), with the Return; Daniel
(167 B.C.), with the Maccabean period.

Let us now look at the historical portions of the Old
Testament. There have been written many Histories of
England; there are in the Old Testament two Histories
of Israel, covering, just like Histories of England, much
the same ground.

I. Taking the narrative portions of the Hexateuch
(see ch. III.), the Books of Judges, Samuel, and Kings, we
have a story, thin in parts, and with many gaps, extending from the earliest times to the Captivity of Judah
(586 B.C.).

II. Taking the Books of Chronicles, Ezra, and
Nehemiah, we have another story, much compressed in
parts, also starting from the earliest times, but, in this
case, reaching to the Reforms of Nehemiah (444–432 B.C.).
To this latter History we may add the Book of Esther,
which purports to relate an episode of the Captivity.

We have thus two narratives which run parallel to
each other down to the Captivity. These narratives
differ from each other pretty much as a General History
of England differs from an Ecclesiastical History. In a
General History ecclesiastical affairs are dealt with only or
chiefly as they bear upon the political and social development. In an Ecclesiastical History the reverse holds
good. This is very roughly the difference between the
two Biblical Histories. The second of the two,
Chronicles—Nehemiah, is, of course, the Ecclesiastical
History.

The dates of these Histories, in their present form,
can be approximately fixed. The History ending with

II. Kings narrates the Captivity of Judah 586 B.C., but does not narrate the Return 538 B.C. It must therefore have been completed at some point between these two dates, that is, during the Captivity. On the other hand, in the Ecclesiastical History not only is the Return narrated, but in I. Chron. iii. we have a genealogical table of the House of David which carries down the genealogy six generations after the Return, that is, to some point in the fourth century B.C. The History must have been completed at that point ; for had the writer or compiler lived later he would certainly have brought the genealogy down to his own later time. The two Histories, then, are separated by some two centuries. Of both Histories the authors are unknown. Tradition indeed has assigned specific names to some of the books; but, with the possible exception of Nehemiah, the books themselves are altogether silent on the question of authorship. Tradition, however, contains one element that is very probably correct, viz., that the earlier History is of prophetic origin. This tradition is preserved in the order in which the books are arranged in the Hebrew Bible. Whereas in our English Bible the books of the Old Testament are arranged in four groups according to their literary forms—Law, History, Poetry, Prophecy,— in the Hebrew Bible they are arranged in three groups— Law, Prophets, Writings or Holy Writings (Hagiographa),—an arrangement marking the three stages in the growth of the Old Testament Canon[1]. In this

---

[1] The Old Testament Canon was not formed at one time. There were three stages in the process of canonization.

1. Pentateuch, canonized latter half of fifth century B.C.

2. Prophets (*including* Joshua, Judges, Samuel, Kings), canonized probably at the end of the third century B.C.

3. Hagiographa (Psalms, Proverbs, Job, Song of Songs, Ruth, Lamentations, Ecclesiastes, Esther, Daniel, Ezra, Nehemiah, Chroni-

grouping the Books of Joshua, Judges, Samuel, Kings, are classed with the Prophets and are called the Former Prophets; Chronicles, Ezra, Nehemiah, Esther, being placed in the Hagiographa. This tradition is in the main borne out by the character of the earlier History, which is imbued with prophetic ideas, and written from the prophetic standpoint. The later History is just as certainly of priestly origin; it is imbued with priestly ideas, and written from the priestly standpoint. This is just what we should expect; our own Ecclesiastical Histories are generally written by priests.

In attempting to estimate the value of these two Histories, that is, the degree in which they fulfil the purpose of all history-writing, we must bear in mind that the function of the historian is twofold: he has to narrate events; and he has to interpret them. Different historians will emphasise one or other side of this two-fold function. One writer will devote himself mainly to narration. With him, therefore, accuracy of detail will be the supreme consideration: he will spend days in clearing up an uncertain date; he will write pages— perhaps a whole monograph—about a disputed name. With another writer, interpretation—the laying bare of the great principles that underlie, and that have been working themselves out in the period he is dealing with —will be the paramount interest. Such a writer will be content with substantial accuracy of detail; he would count it a waste of time to spend days and weeks in ferreting out gossipy details that illustrate no great principle and that had no appreciable influence upon national development.

cles), canonized towards the close   Ryle, *Canon of the Old Testament.*
of the second century B.C.—See

Now there can be little doubt as to which of the two kinds of history-writing is the more valuable. The merely narrative history appeals to, and satisfies, our mere curiosity—our demand to know; the interpretative and philosophic history appeals to, and meets, the demands of our theoretic and practical reason—our desire, that is, to understand as well as to know, and our desire to use the lessons of the past for the guidance of the present.

The qualifications needed for the two kinds of history-writing greatly differ. For mere narrative it is, I suppose, a sufficient equipment to possess average ability, industry, honesty, and to have access to trustworthy sources of information. Given these and a lively style, and you can get an accurate and readable story of past events. For work of this kind special Divine inspiration would be a superfluous endowment. We do not claim such assistance for the writers of our text-books of English History; yet we do not doubt that they give us a substantially true account of the main events of our nation's past. But for the successful interpretation of history, something more than these homely qualifications is needed. A high faith in the rationality of history is needed; for if the historic movement be not rational, it is neither intelligible nor interpretable. So, too, insight is needed—the power to penetrate beneath the surface of things and grasp the hidden and permanent forces, of which events are the fugitive expression. Sympathy, again, is needed: the historian's nature must be in tune with the drama that through the vicissitudes of history is unfolding itself upon the stage of the world.

Now, of the two kinds of history-writing—the predominantly narrative and the predominantly interpretative—Hebrew history belongs emphatically to the latter. The prophetic historians of Israel aim not so much at telling us what happened, as at bringing out the meaning of what happened. History was for them " an orderly " plan, conceived in the counsels of the Eternal slowly " unfolding itself", and it was their delight to trace the principles of the Divine action that they and their fellows might not be mere blind instruments, but conscious fellow-workers with God. Such an aim does not, indeed, entitle the historian to be careless in his handling of events ; but, inasmuch as some events are more central, potent, and decisive than others, the interpretative aim does entitle him to select and arrange his materials so as to set the really significant things of history in bold relief. He may thus wholly neglect, or but slightly notice, much upon which the mere narrator will delight to dwell.

One example will show how little the Hebrew writers cared for mere fulness of detail. The reign of Jeroboam II. was one of the longest in Hebrew annals (782–741 B.C.), and also one of the most splendid: "Israel rose to " a height of prosperity which recalled the palmy days of " Solomon's reign " ; yet the historian dismisses it in six verses (II. Kings xiv. 23–28). This summary notice cannot be due to lack of information ; for the writer lived comparatively near to Jeroboam's time. If a hundred and fifty years hence an English historian, while devoting considerable space to earlier and briefer periods, should dismiss the reign of Victoria in half a dozen sentences, it would certainly be felt that he had some other aim than merely to give information.

Interpretation, then, being the chief aim of the Hebrew historians, the value of their work is to be

estimated by their success or failure in that direction ;
and there, too, we are to look for evidence of their inspiration.

We have seen that for the merely narrative side of
history-writing special Divine aid is not required. We
can get trustworthy narrative without such special aid;
the faculties required for such work are not uncommon.
Nor have we any reason to suppose that in this depart-
ment of their work the Hebrew historians received such
aid ; on the contrary there is much reason to believe they
did not. They themselves make it abundantly clear that
they did not receive their knowledge of the past by any
sort of Divine communication. Like other historians,
they were dependent for such knowledge upon older
documents, many of which they mention by name, for
example, the " Book of Jashar ", the " Book of the Wars
of JEHOVAH ", the " History of Samuel the Seer ", the
" History of Nathan the Prophet ", the " History of Gad
the Seer ", the " Book of the Chronicles of the kings of
Israel ", etc. That those and such-like documents, where
they overlapped, did not always agree, is proved by the
discrepancies which we find in the resultant narrative—
discrepancies which the Biblical historians, through lack
of independent knowledge, either could not reconcile or
did not think it worth while to attempt to reconcile. In
all this they were in just the same position as secular
historians. But just as, notwithstanding, we believe that
secular historians have succeeded in giving us a generally
trustworthy account of the history of Greece or Rome or
England, so we can believe that we have a generally
trustworthy account of the history of Israel. It has,
indeed, been said that if we admit that the historians of
Israel were liable to error in the sphere of narrative, we

have no guarantee that they were not equally liable to it as the interpreters of Divine Revelation. But the objection takes a *doctrinaire* view of revelation, and, as we have seen (p. 49), a *doctrinaire* view of revelation is unbiblical. The claim of the Hebrew historians to be true interpreters of Divine revelation rests upon its own merits, and is to be tested not by their freedom from error in other spheres, but by observation and experience (see pp. 40 ff.).

This interpretative aim of the Hebrew historians greatly relieves, if it does not altogether remove, what, I suppose, is the greatest difficulty presented to ordinary people by modern Criticism, viz., the alleged presence of *myth* and *legend* in the early Biblical records. This difficulty is of course accentuated by our colloquial use of the word *myth* as a synonym for mere fiction. But we must always bear in mind that when scholars speak of a mythical element in the Biblical or any other ancient literature, the colloquial use of the term is not in all their thoughts; and to suppose it to be, would argue the crassest ignorance. Without exception, unless the Hebrew literature be an exception, the earliest literature of all peoples is mythical and legendary. Not until a comparatively late date does it reach the stage of matter-of-fact history. " It begins with individuals either "actual or symbolic who built cities, founded families, "migrated into new lands, gave the first impulse to some "new form of human industry, order, civilisation. Some "of these heroes may have been actual personages, only "showing larger and grander through the mists of ages "than they were in real life. But others, and these are "the more frequent, are purely imaginary, symbolic beings "in whom some popular tradition or feeling more or less "true has embodied itself". Now regarding these myths and legends whether found in Greek, Roman, English, or Maori history, all scholars admit two things. (1) They are not "untrue", if the epithet is intended to express censure. They were the spontaneous product of the imagination; and they were understood literally, and accepted seriously, in those early ages. It is this fact which we, living in a maturer stage of the world's life, find so hard to understand. We can, indeed, admire the early myths and legends as being, many of them, sublime and moving poetry; but we cannot realise the state of mind to which they were sober realities. But the case of our own children may help us. All children are myth-makers and myth-believers. You have only to watch the ways of a little girl with her doll,—the affection she bestows upon it, the dialogues she holds with it, her pleasure if you treat it kindly, her grief if you treat it roughly,—to see how myths are made. To you it is all illusion: to her, at least for the moment, it is all reality. So it was in the world's childhood. Early man, just like the child, could not and did not clearly distinguish between the subjective and the objective, illusion and reality, in his experience. But to describe this mental condition of early man as "untrue" would be as silly as thus to describe the drama of the doll. The wise man knows that the drama of the doll is but the prelude to the loveliest and *truest* thing on earth—the full-grown mother's care for the living child; and the mythopoeic stage of mankind has borne like precious fruit. (2) Nevertheless, the myths of the world's childhood are not historically true: events did not happen so. In fact, a myth is but a parable—a story with a hidden meaning; with this difference that the mythic narrative presents itself not merely as the vehicle of the truth, but as being itself the truth; whereas in the parable, form and essence, husk and kernel, are consciously distinguished. The myth is the parable of the world's childhood; the parable is the myth of the world's maturity.

The myth, then, contains no "fact". The legend, on the other hand, does contain "facts", herein differing from the myth; but "fact" so modified and coloured by thought that it is always difficult, and not seldom impossible, to recover just what really happened (see ch. II.). It thus belongs to a later stage in human development: man is moving on towards the historical stage, but he has not yet reached it.

In myth and legend, then, the "fact" is *nil* or problematical. This being so, they are of little or no value to the historian who is merely an annalist. From the legend he may, indeed, by laborious and skilful questioning, recover some nucleus of historic fact; but of the mythic element he can make no use at all. Far otherwise is it with the philosophic and interpretative historian, for whom "facts" themselves are chiefly valuable as they are significant and embody ideas. For him the myth and legend may be valuable, as I shall try to show, in two ways.

(1) They may already contain true thought—even Divinely given thought. No theist denies that the Spirit of God may communicate with the spirit of man. If thought-transference by telepathy be possible between man and man, how much more possible must it be between the Creator and the creature He has made. Now the human spirit would clothe all such Divinely given thought, as it clothes all its other thoughts, in the modes of expression that are natural to it at any given

9—2

stage of development. But myth and legend are, as we have seen, the modes natural to the earliest stages. Why then should not Divinely given thought be so expressed? I can see no *a priori* reason to the contrary. Human nature is the handiwork of God. It is by His appointment that, both in the individual and in the race, it passes through stages of growth from childhood to maturity. That myth and legend should characterise its childhood, is as much God's ordinance as that scientific history and philosophy should characterise its more mature life. There is, then, no reason why Divine thoughts should not be clothed in the earlier forms of expression. The alternative is, that during the childhood of the race God should have had no communication with man at all; and to the theist this alternative is incredible.

If, then, the myth or legend already embody true and Divine thought, the interpretative historian, who is intent upon the significance of things, especially their Divine significance, can at once adopt it, and work it into that interpretation of the mind of God to man which he also seeks in historical events.

(2) If the myth or legend, as it issues from the mint of the popular mind, have not the impress of true or Divine thought, the interpretative historian can modify it so as to make it the vehicle of such truth, derived by him from other sources. It is of the nature of myth and legend to be plastic. Even in the popular mind they are continually changing. Accordingly, some of the greatest teachers of mankind have been wont to shape them into vehicles of lofty moral teaching. So the Greek tragic poets used the myths and legends of early Greece ; so in the " Idylls of the King " our own Tennyson has used the

Arthurian myth. Now I think that it is chiefly in this latter way the Hebrew historians have used the early Semitic myths and legends. Those historians themselves were not in the mythopoeic stage; but they consciously moulded and adapted the myths and legends which they found in the traditions of their race, so as to make them the vehicles of some of the loftiest teaching in the Bible.

We can, I think, be tolerably certain that this is the true account of the early stories in the Book of Genesis; it certainly is the true account of some of them. Take, for example, the story of the Flood. There are two reasons for believing that in Genesis we have not this story in its earliest form. (1) Since 1872 we have had in our hands the Babylonian story of the Flood. Now between the Biblical account and the Babylonian there are numerous points of resemblance, " too numerous ", says Professor Driver, " and too marked to be due to " accident. The narratives then have evidently a common " origin. And the Hebrew narrative must be *derived* "*from* the Babylonian ; for not only is the Babylonian " story of the Flood much older than (upon any view of " its origin) the Book of Genesis, but the very essence " of the Biblical narrative presupposes a country liable " like Babylonia to inundations ; so that it cannot be " doubted that the story was 'indigenous in Babylonia, " and transplanted to Palestine'". But just as in the Creation narrative, so here, while the material details are similar, in spirit the two stories are far apart as the poles. Thus the Babylonian narrative is grotesquely polytheistic: the gods themselves were affrighted by the catastrophe, and " fled like a pack of hounds "; " they gathered like flies " at the sacrifice offered by the Babylonian Noah when the Flood had ceased. The Hebrew narrative, on the other hand, is "severely monotheistic", and is used as the vehicle of impressive moral and spiritual teaching. The Flood did not historically happen, at least as a universal catastrophe enveloping the globe in a mass of waters many thousand feet deep. But "as the story "is told it becomes...a typical narrative of what is again "and again happening. Again and again, as in the "destruction of Jerusalem, or in the French Revolution, "God's judgements come to men for their sin : again "and again teachers of righteousness are sent to warn of "coming judgement and are ridiculed by a world which "goes on buying and selling, marrying and giving in "marriage, till the flood of God's judgement breaks out "and overwhelms them. Again and again, through these "great judgements there emerges a remnant, a faithful "stock, to be the fountain-head of a new and fresh "development" (*Lux Mundi*, p. xxxvii).

(2) This transformation of the Babylonian myth into a great moral parable might *possibly* have been the work of the general Hebrew mind, working half-unconsciously according to its peculiar bent. But that it is rather to be regarded as the work of the authors or compilers of the Book of Genesis, seems to be shown by the second fact we have to notice, namely, that the story came to the compilers in two forms. Anyone who will carefully examine Gen. vi.—ix. 17 can see for himself that two somewhat differing accounts have been dovetailed together. If you mark with a coloured pencil chs. vi. 5–8 ; vii. 1–5, 7, 10, 12, 16^b, 17, 22, 23 ; viii. 2^b, 3^a, 6^b–13, 20–22, you will make two discoveries : (1) that the marked verses give a fairly connected story ; (2) that the unmarked verses give another fairly con-

nected but somewhat different story, differing in such points as the following: the distribution of clean and unclean animals; the natural causes of the Flood; the duration of the Flood. These two accounts are assigned by critics to the two documents J and P (see pp. 26 ff.). The compiler or compilers, then, so far consciously manipulated the material as to combine two independent accounts, with such pruning of both as such a process entailed. The examination of the story itself, then, enables us to detect at least three stages represented by J, P, and JP combined, by which the Babylonian myth was transformed so as to be the vehicle of a group of impressive moral truths which the Biblical writers had learned elsewhere.

The story of Cain and Abel illustrates the same process. To this story no Babylonian parallel, with which it might be compared, has, as yet, been found. But a study of the story itself shows that it likewise has been consciously modified. As given in Genesis it is manifestly fragmentary and incomplete: elements which at one time it must have contained have been omitted. Thus, we are not told why God preferred Abel's sacrifice to Cain's, nor how the preference was indicated. Two other omissions are concealed by the Authorised Version. In the eighth verse we read : " And Cain told Abel his brother ". This is a mistranslation to get over a difficulty. The correct rendering is " And Cain said unto Abel his brother "; but what is said we are not informed. The Greek version, it is true, fills up the gap by reading " said unto Abel his brother, Let us go into the field ", and some modern scholars accept this reading, holding that it has fallen out of the Hebrew text by mistake. But I cannot help feeling with Bishop

Ryle that this "somewhat vapid sentence" is merely an attempt on the part of the Greek translator to supply an omission already existing in the Hebrew text used by him (*Early Narratives of Genesis,* p. 67). Again, in the fifteenth verse the Authorised Version reads, "And the Lord set a mark upon Cain". This should be rendered, "And the Lord appointed a sign for Cain"; but it is not said in what the sign consisted. Now upon all these points the original story must have given information, for such information is necessary to the completeness of the story, as a story. The explanation of their omission can only be, that the Hebrew writer pruned off elements that were inconsistent with the religious and moral lessons he meant to use the story to convey. What the original drift of the story was, we cannot tell. It may, perhaps, "be traced back to "the recollection, in the people's consciousness, of the "unceasing collision between the agricultural and the "pastoral elements in prehistoric man, and of the domi-"nance asserted by the former" (so Bishop Ryle). But, be that as it may, the Biblical writer has made the story the vehicle of some of the noblest lessons in the Bible. This is not the time to attempt fully to set forth these lessons, but I briefly indicate one or two of them. I must first point out that the seventh verse is mis-translated in the Authorised Version; it should be rendered, "If thou doest well (that is, as the context "demands, cherishest a good inward disposition), shall "there not be lifting up (viz., of the countenance, so that "it will not be downcast and sullen, but bright and "joyous)? And if thou doest not well (cherishest a bad "inward disposition), sin is crouching (like some wild "beast) at the door, and unto thee is its desire (it is

"eager to spring up and overpower thee), but thou
"shouldst rule over it (conquer the rising temptation
"before it is too strong for thee)". How vividly we
have here set forth the progress of sin from the inward
disposition to the outward act, and in particular "the
"danger of harbouring a sullen and unreasoning discon-
"tent". Upon the threshold of such a temper the evil
deed lurks like a beast of prey. It is a powerful enforce-
ment of the ethical principle *Obsta principiis*. Mark,
too, the indissoluble blending of morality and religion :
he who harbours the murderous spirit—who selfishly
asks, Am I my brother's keeper?—is driven out from
the presence of God, a vagabond and a wanderer. It
is a lesson neither the world nor the Church has yet
adequately mastered. And these lessons are quite independent of the fact-value of the narrative by which they
are conveyed. The individual men, Cain and Abel, may
never have existed, but there have been thousands like
them, and the moral of the story is hardly less powerful
than if they had existed. What would be thought of
the man who should argue: "Cain and Abel never
"existed, *therefore* I am in no way responsible for the
"welfare of my brethren"?

So we might go through all the stories in the early
chapters of Genesis and show how the Hebrew writers
have freely adapted them to their own purposes. This
fact seems to me to show that these writers attached
little value to these stories as records of events; for
they must have been aware that in refashioning them,
as they did, they were destroying such value.

But when we have pointed out isolated moral and
spiritual lessons of which these stories have been made
the vehicle, we have not adequately described the use

made of them by the Hebrew writers. The Hebrew writers did not forget that they were, above all else, historians. Accordingly they did not content themselves, as merely ethical and religious teachers might have been content, with simply using these stories to teach isolated lessons. If they could not use them as history, they could yet use them in the interest of that interpretation of history which it is their purpose subsequently to give. Accordingly, what we find in the early chapters of Genesis is not simply a number of edifying moral truths, but a statement of certain great outstanding features of human history. Let us look at the stories from this point of view. Notwithstanding the fashionable optimism, resting upon a mistaken application of the doctrine of evolution, " the most impressive fact in human history is sin "—human nature's tendency, often operative on a vast scale, towards deterioration. This tendency has been operative in human history as far back as we can trace. Well ; the Hebrew historian uses the Eden tradition to represent the sin-tendency as manifesting itself along with the first beginnings of the race. Yet at the same time it is declared that man will never, for long, come to terms with sin ; but will wage with it ever-renewed warfare, to be crowned at last with victory[1].

Next, the story of Cain and Abel is used to portray some of sin's darkest historical embodiments. Next, the tradition as to the rise of civilisation and the arts is used to show how sin has mingled with the process ; and Lamech, brandishing the newly invented sword, and

[1] The Eden story is almost certainly Babylonian in origin, though no Babylonian parallel has as yet been discovered. Eden is a Babylonian place name; Hiddekel (Tigris) and Euphrates are Babylonian rivers; the Tree of Life and the Cherubim are Babylonian conceptions.

boasting to his wives that in it he possesses the means of an ampler revenge than was vouchsafed to Cain, is the impersonation, not yet out of date, of a sin-stained civilisation using its resources for purposes of destruction :—

> "Adah and Zillah, hear my voice ;
> Ye wives of Lamech, hearken to my speech ;
> Verily I slay a man for (merely) wounding me,
> And a young man for (merely) bruising me.
> If Cain shall be avenged sevenfold,
> Truly Lamech seventy and sevenfold".

The story of the Flood, as we have seen, is used to illustrate the Divine reactions, in judgement, mercy, and redemption, evoked by sin in human history. Finally, the story of the Tower of Babel (manifestly of Babylonian origin or suggestion, though no Babylonian parallel is as yet known) furnishes the occasion for reflections upon another great outstanding factor in human history, viz., the differentiation of a race, one in its origin, into a variety of peoples and languages. On the one hand, this differentiation presents itself to the writer as an evil. " The separation of mankind into peoples", says Dr Dillmann, " must decidedly be regarded as an evil, " when there is no higher bond binding them all together, " or when such is no longer in existence. It hinders " common undertakings, and is the source of all inter- " national strife with its innumerable evil consequences. " But diversity of language confirms and perpetuates the " existing opposition. Diversity of language leads to " diversity in mental processes and modes of thought, " and the inner mental difference in respect of ideals and " ways of regarding things becomes still greater". On the other hand, he perceives that this diversity is also a good: it puts a check upon the monstrous development of evil which might ensue, were all peoples able easily to unite in endeavours often selfish and vain. But he further perceives that it is not the final state of the human race. Already he has in view that Divine movement in history whereby one people shall be selected to be the germ of the Kingdom of God, in which eventually all peoples and languages will find their bond of unity in a common faith in One God, All-holy and All-loving, and in obedience to His voice; and so the story of the Tower of Babel is immediately followed by the Call of Abraham, in whom all the families of the earth shall be blessed. Such then is the use made by the Hebrew historians of the early myths of their race. They might, with *naïve* simplicity, have accepted them in all the crudity and grotesqueness in which they found them. They might have rejected them as wholly worthless. They might have taken infinite pains to extract from them some uncertain modicum of fact. They did none of these things; but did what I cannot but think was far better: they freely refashioned them so as to make them vehicles of lofty moral teaching, and, also, so as to give vivid expression, by way of preface to the subsequent history, to some of the great problems with which all earnest students of human history must grapple:—

> "The picture writing of the world's grey seers,
> The myths and parables of the primal years,
> Whose letter kills, by them[1] interpreted
> Take healthful meanings fitted to our needs".

The question then is just this,—Is this moral and philosophical teaching true to human experience? If it

---

[1] I have taken the liberty of substituting this word for Whittier's "Thee".

is, the presence of myth and legend in the Bible is justified. And further the Biblical writers are shown to have possessed a true insight into human life and history. Now of this insight inspiration is an adequate and, as I believe, by far the most probable, explanation.

But we must not exaggerate the mythic element in the early Biblical records. Some scholars would resolve the whole patriarchal story into a series of myths. Abraham, Isaac, Jacob, Esau, and the rest, it is said, never existed in flesh and blood. They are but mythical representations of the inter-relations and fortunes of tribes and peoples. There may be some truth in this theory. Jacob, Esau, Joseph, though not Abraham, are frequently used as tribal and national names. The tribes of Ephraim and Manasseh are often called Joseph; the Edomites, Esau; and the whole Hebrew people, Jacob or Israel (the patriarch's second name). But when the theory is stated in such a form as to sweep all the patriarchs into the region of mythology, it is difficult to receive it. Most people, I think, will be disposed to agree with Professor Driver's view : " The abundance of " personal incident and detail in the patriarchal narratives " as a whole seems to constitute a serious objection to "this explanation of their meaning : would the move- " ments of tribes be represented in this veiled manner on " such a large scale as would be the case if this expla- " nation were the true one " ? Mr Stopford Brooke, who, though not an expert in Biblical criticism, has yet a fine literary tact, takes the same view : " Nor can I think, in " spite of some modern criticism, that Joseph, Jacob and " the rest were originally only the names of tribes before " they became the names of national heroes. I do not " think that we are licensed wholly to deny that these

" men may have existed as real personages, and that the "stories grew out of their lives" (*The Old Testament and Modern Life*, p. 10). That the story has been idealised, that is, interpreted with a fine feeling for what was true and beautiful in the patriarchal character, however imperfectly expressed in their lives, and for the dealings of God with them, so as to make it vividly appeal to the imagination, the heart, the conscience, the will, of ordinary men, we may, indeed, well believe. Such idealisation would be in harmony with the interpretative character of Hebrew history-writing in general. But to regard such idealisation as falsification would be as absurd as to regard the landscape-painting of a great artist as a falsification of nature. It is simply to bring out in vivid and splendid colours the beauty that is there, but that is unperceived by the coarser and duller feelings of common men.

I have now said enough to indicate the bearing of an alleged mythic and legendary element in the Bible upon the question of inspiration. I cannot think that the recognition of such an element forbids belief in the reality of that form of inspiration which, on independent grounds, we have seen reason to adopt.

CHAPTER IX

WE pass now to the prophetic interpretation of history proper.

I. With unparalleled clearness the Hebrew historians saw God—living, personal, self-conscious, self-determining Mind and Will—present and active in human history. For most of us, the only real factors in history are man with his schemes and Nature as his helper or antagonist. God, if we think of Him at all, is a pale abstraction. To the Hebrew historians the reverse was true; God was the supremely Real and Vital. No men ever had such a vivid perception of the reality, the livingness, the greatness, the energy of God. Whenever we would have our blanched conception of God freshened we must still go to the Old Testament writers; read, for example, Is. xl. 12–31.

It never occurred to these men to prove the existence of God. Such an idea would have seemed to them the last extreme of absurdity. They were living and moving in the midst of His operations. He was present in all the movements of Nature and History, initiating them and winding them up,—"the First and the Last".

"The thing that is done upon the earth, He doeth it Himself". This vivid realisation of the activity of God appears in the specific Hebrew name for God—JEHOVAH[1] (JAHAVEH). The origin of this name is obscure: but its meaning in the historic religion of Israel is determined for us by Ex. iii., vi. Moses has asked by what name he shall speak of God to his enslaved countrymen. He is bidden to say, I WILL BE[2] hath sent me. A further formula is also given—I WILL BE WHAT I WILL BE (not, "I am that I am"), of which I WILL BE is, doubtless, an abbreviation. JAHAVEH is simply the third person singular of the verb; "He will be" naturally being used when another is speaking of God, as the first person naturally is used by God Himself. As to the force of this name, "it is a historic formula; "it refers not to what God will be in Himself; it is no "prediction regarding His Nature, but one regarding "what He will approve Himself to others, regarding "what He will show Himself to be". It affirms that what God will be (and that will ever be receiving fresh content from ever-fresh manifestations of Him) He *will* be,—will approve Himself to be without fail. The meaning will be more clearly seen, if we slightly alter the order of the words: "That which I will be I will

---

[1] JEHOVAH is a mongrel form in which the vowels of the Hebrew word for "Lord" are combined with the consonants (JHVH) of the Hebrew Proper Name of God in order to indicate that, in reading and speaking, the former word is to be substituted for the latter. This substitution was due to the superstitious dread of uttering the Divine Proper Name which prevailed in later Judaism. JAHAVEH is probably the correct pronunciation.

[2] See R.V. margin. I AM of the A.V. is a mistranslation. Moreover it imports a metaphysical idea foreign to Hebrew thought. It is derived from the Greek Version and shows the influence of the Greek mind. "The verb *to be* in Hebrew hardly "expresses the idea of absolute or "self-existence: it rather expresses "what *is* or *will be* historically" (Davidson).

indeed be". The construction is similar to that in
Ex. xxxiii. 19, "I will have mercy on whom I will have
mercy", which is an emphatic affirmation that on whom
God will have mercy He will indeed have mercy
(Davidson, *Old Testament Theology*, pp. 45 ff.; Robertson
Smith, *Prophets of Israel*, p. 385). JEHOVAH, then, is
God energising and manifesting Himself in history.   In
fact "history is JEHOVAH in operation".

This vivid realisation by Israel's historians of God as
the Strong One energising in history may, perhaps,
explain much of the so-called miraculous in the Old
Testament, which is so great a stumbling-block to many
moderns.   As we read the stupendous miracles of the
Exodus and of the Lawgiving at Sinai, we cannot help
asking, Had we been there should we have seen these
"wonders in the land of Ham" or heard "the voice of
a trumpet exceeding loud"?

Now I do not propose to discuss the general question
of the miraculous.   By all theists miracle must be
regarded as antecedently possible, and, if there be
sufficient reason for it, also probable.   But the question
is, whether, in such cases as those we are considering, the
historian meant to record miracle,—whether he meant
us to understand that things happened just as he has
narrated them.   And it is possible that he did not mean
this, and that he would have been much surprised that
anyone should imagine him to mean this.   It is possible
that we have here an idealisation of history similar to
the idealisation of character which we found in Genesis.
To idealise is not, we must remember, imaginatively to
put into things powers and qualities that are not already
there; on the contrary it is imaginatively to bring out
into clear light what is already there, but is unperceived

by the superficial observer.   Now miracles are not
scattered indiscriminately over the pages of the Old
Testament; much of the narrative is as "natural" as
that of any book of ordinary history.   Miracles are, for
the most part, grouped around certain great crises, such
as the Exodus and the giving of the Law.   Now, in all
such crises the historian felt that there was a special
intervention of God; and in so feeling all theists must
believe that the historian was profoundly right.   The
liberation of Israel from Egyptian serfdom, however
accomplished, was, undoubtedly, a decisive event in the
higher life of mankind, which the theist must ascribe to
the Providence of God; the Moral Law, however communicated to man, the theist must trace ultimately to
God.   Now, at a more primitive stage of religion such
natural phenomena as plague, tempest, thunder, earthquake were regarded as being, in a special sense, acts of
God and tokens of His presence.   It was natural then
that the historian, when he wished specially to emphasise
the action of God in human history, should make a
symbolic use of these phenomena for the purpose.   He
might have contented himself with saying, It was God
Who delivered our fathers out of Egypt.   It was God
Who gave us the Moral Law.   But would he by such
language have brought the Divine fact home to the men
of his own day—to the men of any day—as vividly as he
has brought it home by the splendid and awe-inspiring
portrayal of the plagues in Egypt and of the thunders
and lightnings of Sinai[1]?   I do not assert that the entire

[1] It is not denied that the story
of the ten plagues may rest upon a
basis of fact. Such phenomena were
not unknown in Egypt (see art.,
"Plagues of Egypt", in Hastings'
Bible Dictionary).   It   is   their
severity, rapid succession and prediction by Moses that raise the ten
plagues above the plane of "the
natural".

miraculous element in the Old Testament is to be explained in this symbolic fashion; but that much of it is to be explained in this way, cannot, I think, be denied. The opening verses of the Eighteenth Psalm are a classic example. This Psalm, whether written by David or by another, is meant to express David's experiences. The first part of it celebrates his deliverance from his many perils of death. Those deliverances were profoundly felt to be due to the intervening Providence of God, and this Divine intervention is described thus :—

> "In my distress I called upon the LORD,
> And cried unto my God :
> He heard my voice out of His temple,
> And my cry before Him came into His ears.
> Then the earth shook and trembled,
> The foundations also of the mountains moved
> And were shaken, because He was wroth.
> *   *   *   *   *   *   *
> He bowed the heavens also, and came down ;
> And thick darkness was under His feet.
> *   *   *   *   *   *   *
> The LORD also thundered in the heavens,
> And the Most High uttered His voice ;
> Hailstones and coals of fire.
> And he sent out His arrows, and scattered them ;
> Yea, lightnings manifold, and discomfited them.
> *   *   *   *   *   *   *
> He sent from on high, He took me ;
> He drew me out of many waters.
> He delivered me from my strong enemy".

Now we have the history of David in our hands, including the narrative of his many perils and escapes, and no such miraculous phenomena are recorded. Nevertheless it was indeed God Who had preserved him ; and the Psalm seeks to bring out this fact by the symbolic use of natural phenomena raised to the height of miracle[1].

This, then, is what I mean by the idealisation of history—the heightening of it in order vividly to bring home to the imagination the presence and activity of God. And this way of treating history is due to the historian's own vivid realisation of that presence and activity.

II. The historians of Israel saw that the God Who energises in history is Righteous. He has a fixed character of His own. He is the Upholder, the Avenger, the Rewarder, of right doing and right relations among men. The historian's own conception of right might be crude, and might show the limitations of his age, but he was sure that whatever was right had God for its strong Helper. So he believed that might was right; not in the immoral sense that right does not matter so long as you have might, but in the high moral sense that right is the one omnipotent thing.

As we have already (ch. v.) considered the prophetic conception of God, it is unnecessary to pursue the subject.

III. Apprehending God as a living and righteous Power operating in history, the prophetic historians saw *purpose* in history. They were the first to conceive a philosophy of history. Underlying, pervading, guiding that wrestling mass of conflicting natural and human forces, which is what history seems to most men, they saw an orderly Divine plan unfolding itself. All the great movements of history—the migrations of peoples, the rise and fall of empires—were steps in the evolution

---

[1] For other examples see Is. xiii. 10; xxxiv. 4; Ezek. xxxii. 7, 8; Amos viii. 9. See also, the chapter on "The Symbolism of the Bible" in Professor Sanday, *The Life of Christ in Recent Research*.

of a great purpose. The perception of this purpose did not lead them, as it might easily have led them, to regard men as mere automata. They believed in human freedom ; they believed that men formed genuine purposes and carried them out; they believed, therefore, in human responsibility. The proof lies in their whole-hearted denunciation of sin. But they saw something moving forward in the individual life and in the general movements of mankind, that men did not devise, and that yet had certainly the nature of purpose. God never for a moment lets go the sovereignty of the world, but in some way, above human comprehension, the schemes and doings of men and nations are caught up into, and made to subserve, His Divine purposes ; just as in the natural sphere the total result of any act of ours is not solely, perhaps not at all, what we intend, but what the forces of nature, which are independent of us, permit. This great conception of a Divine Drama of history (and we owe it to the Biblical historians) does for the phenomena of historic time what the law of gravitation does for the bodies in space: it binds them into a rational and systematic unity.

IV. Nor are the Biblical writers in the dark as to what the Divine purpose is,—the goal towards which human history irresistibly moves. That goal is the complete realisation of the Kingdom of God. This of course follows from the preceding three ideas.

If a Righteous God be the supreme Factor in history, and if He be working out a purpose there, that purpose can be no other than the realisation of His Kingdom. The Kingdom of God is the theme of the whole Bible ; it is that which gives this collection of diverse books, whose composition embraces a thousand years, its mar-

vellous unity. According to the Bible the universe is
the theatre (this, and not any scientific interest, is why
the Bible begins with creation), and history the progressive realisation, of the Kingdom of God.

I do not propose to trace the development of the
idea of the Kingdom of God in the Old Testament, but
simply to state the highest conception there reached[1].
The Kingdom of God, then, is the moral and spiritual
community in which the Divine Will is freely accepted
and realised, and in which, seeing that the Divine Will
is essentially beneficent, man enjoys all the good of
which his nature is susceptible. The Kingdom is thus
essentially a social conception. It involves a double
fellowship—a fellowship Divine and human. On the
one hand, it is fellowship—expressing itself in free
obedience, dependence, homage, thanksgiving, prayer—
of man with God, and of God, in self-communicating
grace, with man. On the other hand, it is fellowship,
expressing itself in fulness of ethical life, among men
who stand in the same relation to God. So closely are
these two fellowships united in the Biblical view, as
being but different aspects of one reality, that in the
original language the Bible uses one and the same word

---

[1] For the full conception of the Kingdom we must, of course, go to the New Testament. We must, however, never forget that neither in the Old Testament nor in the New is the Kingdom a merely ideal creation, projected wholly into the future. Already in the national life of Israel the Kingdom had an in-choate embodiment. Israel was constituted a theocratic State, i.e. a Kingdom of God (Ex. xix. 5, 6). JEHOVAH was the true King. The human depositaries of power were but His representatives and vice-gerents. The laws and institutions of the State, as well civil as eccle-siastical, were the expressions and embodiments of His Will. It was the imperfection of its present national form that stirred the prophets to long for, and to struggle after, its more perfect realisation in the future. With the Advent of the Christ and the founding of the Church, the Kingdom cast off its national limitations, and entered upon that career of world-wide conquest in the midst of which we ourselves are living.

—"chāsīd"—to denote the man who stands in devout relations to God, and the man who stands in true ethical relations to his fellow men. It is this conception of the Kingdom, as uniting God and man in one moral and spiritual community, which explains that fusion of religion and morality which is the great characteristic of Biblical teaching. In the Kingdom a man cannot serve God without serving his generation, and he cannot serve his generation without serving God. By morality religion is saved from becoming vague and dreamy; by religion morality is saved from becoming thin and conventional[1].

By the rank and file the Kingdom was, perhaps, regarded as the exclusive privilege of the Jew[2], but the highest prophets had visions of its world-wide sway,— the goal, not of Israelitish, but of human history. This Kingdom is presented in the Bible as the *summum bonum*—the supreme gift of God to man and the supreme object of human endeavour. Though the contrary has often been asserted, the Bible knows nothing of a merely individual good,—of a good for man apart from his fellows, either here or hereafter. Not that the Bible is careless of the single life, and careful only of the type; on the contrary, it is in the Bible that the individual first comes to his rights. But the truth, sometimes regarded as the discovery of modern ethics, that the individual reaches his best life only in and through his fellows, is already recognised in the Bible; save that the Bible goes beyond modern ethics in grounding the fellowship of man with man upon fellowship of all with God. It was through this conception of the Kingdom

[1] "It follows that he who sins "against human society sins against "God. Ancient Israel knew only "sins and no crimes".—Cornill, *Prophets of Israel*, p. 25.

[2] The predominant conception of later Judaism.

as the goal of history that the Biblical writers attained the assurance of the immortality of the individual.

We must consider this subject somewhat in detail. Nothing, I suppose, in the Old Testament is more perplexing to a thoughtful reader, who is at the same time a Christian believer, than its attitude towards the question of a future life. Thus, throughout the entire historical books life with God in the unseen world is spoken of in connexion with two men only—Enoch and Elijah; and these are represented not as surviving death, but as escaping it. With these two exceptions, though the deaths of patriarchs, law-givers, priests, prophets, kings, warriors, are recorded, though they are lamented and buried, not a word is spoken regarding any hope for the future. This silence is strange in writers so intensely religious as the Hebrew historians. You shall best appreciate its strangeness, if you compare David's Elegy over Saul and Jonathan with the great Elegies of our own Literature—*Lycidas, Adonais, In Memoriam.* Even the sceptical Shelley cannot refrain from words of faith and hope :—

> "He hath awakened from the dream of life.
> *   *   *   *   *   *
> He hath outsoared the shadow of our night.
> Envy and calumny and hate and pain,
> And that unrest which men miscall delight,
> Can touch him not and torture not again.
> From the contagion of the world's slow stain
> He is secure ; and now can never mourn
> A heart grown cold, a head grown grey in vain.
> *   *   *   *   *   *
> He lives, he wakes—'tis Death is dead, not he ".

Not less significant is the silence of the Book of Proverbs. That Book is taken up wholly with maxims for the guidance of conduct. One would expect such a book to make much use of so powerful a motive as is afforded by the truth of personal immortality. But, in truth, this motive is not once appealed to. There is not a word about using this life as a preparation for another and endless life. The horizon of the Book of Proverbs is limited by this present life, and its wisdom is a wisdom of this present life only.

But stranger still than silence are the passages in which a future life seems to be categorically denied :—

"The grave cannot praise Thee;
 Death cannot celebrate Thee :
 They that go down into the pit cannot hope for Thy truth.
 The living, the living, he shall praise Thee, as I do this day:
 The father to the children shall make known Thy truth".
 (Is. xxxviii. 18, 19.)

"Hear my prayer, O LORD,
 And give ear unto my cry ;
 Hold not Thy peace at my tears :
 For I am but a guest with Thee,
 And a sojourner, as all my fathers were.
 O spare me, that I may recover brightness,
 Before I go hence, and be no more". (Ps. xxxix. 12 f.)

"Cast off among the dead,
 Like the slain that lie in the grave,
 Whom Thou rememberest no more ;
 And they are cut off from Thy hand". (Ps. lxxxviii. 5.)

"For to him that is joined with all the living there "is hope : for a living dog is better than a dead lion. . . . "But the dead know not anything, neither have they "any more a reward ; for the memory of them is for- "gotten. . . . Whatsoever thy hand findeth to do, do it "with thy might ; for there is no work, nor device, nor

"knowledge, nor wisdom, in the grave, whither thou
"goest" (Eccles. ix. 4, 5, 10).

There are other passages of like tone.

Now how are we to explain this silence and this
denial? Well, it is to be explained as a transitional
stage in the growth of Hebrew religion. We have seen
that the early Hebrews shared the beliefs of the other
Semitic peoples. According to those beliefs the gods
were purely tribal or national deities. Each tribe had
its god, who was concerned wholly with tribal affairs.
He had no dealings with individuals as such, but only
with the tribe as a whole. It was the tribal existence
that the divine honour was concerned to maintain ; that
being secured, the fate of the individual mattered little.

As a tribal god his jurisdiction was confined to the
tribal territory. He was a god of the upper world, and
of a limited portion of this upper world, viz., the portion
occupied by his worshippers. As he had no dealings
with the individual, the fate of the individual beyond
death did not concern him. He was not regarded as
having any jurisdiction beyond the grave. Nevertheless
the heathen Semites believed intensely that men survived death. They believed that the spirits of the dead
possessed a high degree of activity ; that they were
cognisant of what happened upon earth ; that they had
a knowledge of the future ; that they could interfere in
mundane affairs to help or to injure. Over this unseen
realm the tribal god was not conceived to have any
jurisdiction. Men lived in families there, and the beings
who held sway were not the gods, but the Heads of
families. Accordingly, to the public worship of the
tribal god, the early Semite added a domestic worship
of Ancestors. Each family had its household gods, to

whom sacrifices were offered, by which it was thought that the spirits of the dead were not merely honoured but also nourished. If this worship were not duly paid, they would, it was believed, inflict injury upon their living descendants. It was they, and not the god, who were consulted about the future ; it was they, and not the god, who controlled the fates of individuals. In this realm of the dead it was not believed that there were any moral distinctions. The good and the bad mingled promiscuously. There were no Heaven and Hell. Morality being simply tribal law and custom, violations of it were punished here on earth, not beyond. The unseen world was a non-moral world[1]. Such was the general Semitic belief regarding the future life, and the early Hebrews shared it. Now when the differentiation of Hebrew religion from Semitic paganism began, it was not completed all at once ; it was not completed, indeed, till the advent of Christ. The first step—but a step which carried with it all the mighty future—was the differentiation of JEHOVAH'S character from that of other Semitic deities. He came to be regarded as a God of righteousness, justice, purity. But He was still thought of as a tribal god, concerned not with the individual, but with the tribe or nation. His sway was still conceived as limited to this upper world. Thus at first the Hebrew differed from his Semitic kinsman only in having as his national god, a god of righteousness, justice, purity. In other respects his beliefs were the same. For him, too, JEHOVAH had no sway over the world beyond death. For him, too, that world was a non-moral world ; retribution was confined to this life.

[1] Our modern disbelief in future retribution is simply a reversion to Semitic paganism.

He, too, had his domestic worship of Ancestors, along-side of his public worship of JEHOVAH. He, too, believed that his ancestors could help or injure him. He, too, consulted them in times of difficulty. But from the moment that Israel came to think of JEHOVAH as a righteous God, the death-knell of this non-moral, heathen conception of the unseen world was sounded ; though it took centuries for the people as a whole to realise the essential antagonism of the two conceptions. But as time passed on, under the rule of a moral deity, they did realise it.   It became more and more impossible for them to conceive of a non-moral world.   As they came to believe that, here and now, prosperity and adversity depended upon moral causes, it became more and more impossible for them to believe in the capricious inter-ference of departed ancestors.   As they realised more and more the power of JEHOVAH, they more and more ceased to believe that there could be any other power in human affairs than His.   The whole system of ancestor-worship became repugnant.   At last it was forbidden by law, and many of the enactments of Hebrew law, which to those who have not the key seem unintelligible, e.g., the laws regarding mourning for the dead,—are directed against it.   But, now, let us note carefully just what happened.   The growing moralization of the Hebrew under the sway of JEHOVAH's righteousness and justice and purity, did not simply lead him to cast away the non-moral elements in his belief regarding the world beyond, leaving him still in possession of his belief in the *fact* that the human spirit survived death.   No ; as so often happens, the association of ideas was too strong. A future life seemed to him so bound up and identified with the heathen conception of it, that when he found himself no longer able to accept the latter, he at the same time abandoned the former. Even in our own day many people cannot distinguish between the essence of a belief and the particular embodiment of the essential idea, which they have inherited, and to which they have long been accustomed. For example, the essential fact that the universe has a rational and spiritual Source was, down to our own time, associated in men's minds with the conception that the universe, as we know it, was created in six days. When Science proved that this was not so,—that the universe, as we know it, is the result of an age-long evolution—what did many people do? Did they merely change their view of God's creative method and say, We had thought that He had wrought by the method of instantaneous creation ; we now know that He works by the method of evolution? Not at all. So bound up with the instantaneous method was their conception of God's activity, that, when they abandoned the one, they abandoned the other, and ceased to believe that God had wrought at all, or that the universe had any rational and spiritual ground[1]. So likewise the ancient Hebrews. So bound up with heathen conceptions was their belief in a life after death, that, when they could no longer believe those conceptions, they ceased to believe in such a life altogether. This then is the explanation of that disbelief in a future life which is so marked and puzzling a feature of the Old Testament. *The belief was killed by Ethical Monotheism.* But this was only a stage, not a finality ; the destruction which precedes a nobler reconstruction. So essential was it

---

[1] A closer parallel is the modern disbelief in a future life, due, at least in part, to our inability any longer to believe in the materialistic heaven and hell with which that life has been closely associated in our minds.

that every trace of heathenism should be removed before
a pure and lofty conception of the future could be communicated, that even the idea of a future life itself must
be swept away.   The religion of JEHOVAH would build
a completely new structure of human hope, to which
heathenism should contribute nothing, upon foundations
essentially moral and spiritual.   If it seems strange to
us that the Divine Educator of Israel should allow so
practically important a truth as that of personal immortality to fall into abeyance, even if only for a time,
we must remember that, in the wisdom of the same
Educator, the disbelief was not without compensations.
Though the Hebrew lost his faith in a future life, he did
not lose his faith in JEHOVAH.   JEHOVAH was still his
God, and fellowship with JEHOVAH was still his *summum
bonum*.   His disbelief in the future compelled him to
seek to realise that fellowship here and now, within the
bounds of this earthly life.   He thus learned that life
could be lived with God here and now, and was thus
saved from that undue depreciation of this life's moral
and spiritual possibilities, which a too vivid realisation
of the future life has sometimes fostered in the Christian
Church.   It may be that the eclipse of faith in immortality in our own day is meant to teach some analogous
lesson.

But in reformations it often happens that there are
those who never get beyond the destructive stage, when
the old is overthrown ; who mistake what is really preparatory for what is final.   Even so was it in Israel.
There were those, represented in the Gospels by the
Sadducees, who, failing to see that the period of denial
was only preparatory to a nobler affirmation, exalted
the provisional denial of a future life into an article of

faith permanently valid[1]. But the Divine Education of
Israel went on, and even within the Old Testament the
faith in a future life is morally and spiritually reborn.
And it is reborn in connexion with the conception of
the Kingdom of God. The new faith in immortality,
derived from the conception of the Kingdom of God,
first appears in a passage which forms part of our
present Book of Isaiah, but which many modern
scholars assign to a much later date. This question
of date is for our purpose entirely unimportant. The
passage forms part of the Old Testament, and it is what
is actually found in the Old Testament, by whomsoever
and whensoever written, that we are investigating. The
passage in question is Is. xxvi. 19 :—

"Thy dead men (Israel!) shall arise, and the inhabitants of the
"dust shall awake and shout for joy ; for a dew of lights is thy dew,
"and the earth shall produce the shades".

"The writer looks forward to the setting up of the
"Kingdom, to the city of strength whose walls and
"bulwarks are salvation, and whose gates are open that
"the righteous nation may enter in (xxvi. 1, 2). And
"since the nation was but few in number, the righteous
"dead shall arise and share the blessedness of the re-
"generate nation" (xxvi. 19).

It was not mere sentiment that gave birth to this
hope that those who had lived and suffered in the
imperfect past would live again to share the blessedness
of the perfect future, in restored fellowship with God
and the righteous community. A profound logic was,

---

[1] They have their modern coun-
terparts in those persons who,
accepting the destructive work of
modern criticism as final, have
abandoned Christianity, failing to
realise that destruction is merely
preparatory to a nobler reconstruction.

implicitly if not explicitly, at work in the prophet's mind. Let us see what this logic was. Though the Kingdom is already present in the world wherever men are living a true religious and ethical life, yet in its full scope and beneficence it is a thing of the future,—the final goal, not the present content, of human history. The question then must sooner or later arise, Who are to enjoy the perfect Divine-human social order? Shall only those enjoy it who shall happen to be living when the perfect order comes,—the latest-born of men? This is a profoundly important question, for upon the answer it depends whether we shall regard the cosmic process as moral or as immoral. If only those born latest in time are destined to enjoy the perfect social order, then it would seem that the cosmic process must be pronounced immoral. For the fundamental principle of morality is, that man—each and every man—being a moral personality, must never be treated as a mere instrument—a mere means to an end, but always as an end in himself, however, in a subordinate way, he may also be instrumental. Everybody must count as one, and nobody as more than one. This is just what distinguishes a man from a thing: thing is instrument; man is end. It is the violation of this principle that is the source of all oppression, injustice, cruelty, lust. All such evils arise from our treating our fellows as mere instruments of our profit or pleasure,—from our forgetting that every man is to be regarded as an end. Now if the perfect social order, which, however we conceive it, is manifestly a thing of the distant future, is to be the exclusive heritage of those who shall be alive at its advent, then on a tremendous scale the cosmic process has been using, is using, for ages will continue to use,

innumerable millions of the human race—the overwhelming majority in fact—who have been toiling to
bring on the better future, while they themselves have
endured the evils of the imperfect present, as mere
means to an end entirely beyond themselves, which
they shall never see,—mere instruments of a good to
be enjoyed by a favoured few, whose only merit is that
they are the latest born :—

> "And if there be this Promised Land indeed,
>   Our children's children's children's heritage,
> Oh, what a prodigal waste of precious seed,
>   Of myriad myriad lives from age to age,
>   Of woes and agonies and blank despairs,
> Through countless cycles, that some fortunate heirs
> May enter, and conclude the pilgrimage"!

If such is the meaning of the cosmic process, then
the cosmic process must be pronounced immoral to the
core. It has been using countless moral personalities as
mere instruments, that is, as mere things. In such a
world the creation of moral personality is the refinement
of cruelty. If the cosmic process is to be conceived as
moral,—and it is essential to our moral health that it
should be so conceived,—the Kingdom of God—the
perfect order of human life—cannot belong to a single
generation, but must be the heritage of all mankind.
To secure that it shall be so, two things are required:
(1) the immortality of the individual in order that those
who have laboured and suffered that succeeding generations might attain a richer and fuller life, may have
their part in the final consummation[1]; (2) that not this
earth, which is destined to be resolved into the elements
out of which it was formed, but the unseen world be

---

[1] Materialistic Socialism robs the individual of this most righteous hope.

the final sphere of the perfected Kingdom. Both these postulates, which come to full expression in the New Testament, are already nascent in the Old Testament (Is. xxvi. 19; li. 16; lxv. 17; Ps. cii. 25 ff.)[1].

The account here given of the genesis and meaning of the Biblical doctrine of immortality, meets two objections often alleged against that doctrine. (1) Persons of a materialistic bent, having satisfied themselves that belief in a future life—admittedly wide-spread in all ages of which we have any knowledge—originated in a mistaken interpretation by primitive man of the phenomena of dreams, and regarding the Biblical doctrine as being merely a local variety of the general belief, have thought that, the general belief being discredited by its crude origin, the Biblical doctrine necessarily falls with it. Whether, even if we grant the dream-theory of origin, the general belief is thereby discredited, I shall not stay to enquire; though it is well to remember that a thinker so strong and scientific as John Fiske did not think that what he calls "this supreme poetic achievement of man—his belief in his own immortality", was invalidated by this supposed origin[2]. But, as we have seen, the specifically Biblical doctrine did not, historically, thus originate. The primitive belief came to be wholly rejected by the Hebrew people. There was a period of complete scepticism or rather disbelief. When the belief reappeared, it was a new faith resting on far other foundations than the early Semitic paganism, being wholly derived, by a moral and spiritual logic, from the peculiarly Hebrew conception of the Kingdom of God. To discredit the Biblical doctrine of immortality,

---

[1] See Prof. Brown, *Christian Theology in Outline*, p. 419.
[2] *Everlasting Life*, p. 18 ff.

it is futile to talk of the ghostly fancies of dreaming savages; you must discredit the whole conception of the Kingdom of God. (2) The second charge is that the Biblical doctrine fosters selfishness. This charge is without foundation. As we have already seen the Bible knows nothing of a good for the individual wholly apart from his fellows, either here or hereafter. What is promised to the individual is a share in the perfect life of the Kingdom of God :—

> "For *there* the LORD hath commanded the blessing,
> Even life for evermore".

The selfishness and self-centredness which, it must be allowed, have sometimes been associated with the hope of immortality, are an intrusion of Greek thought, wholly alien from the Hebrew mind. According to Greek thought "the soul was not only immortal but "eternal, alike without beginning and end, and it was "capable of repeated incarnations in human and animal "bodies. From this doctrine it follows that the present "environment of the soul is only one of the many in "which it exists from age to age, and accordingly this "community or that has no abiding significance. Such "a soul can only consider God and itself. In Israel, "however, the soul was not in itself immortal, but only "won immortality through life in God[1]", and, as we have seen, life in God was indissolubly bound up with life in the Divine community or Kingdom of God. The Biblical doctrine of immortality is not a concession to selfishness,

---

[1] Prof. Charles' *Eschatology Hebrew, Jewish and Christian*. To this book I am much indebted. Re-incarnation as taught by modern Theosophy involves the same extreme individualism as the ancient Greek conception.

but a recognition of the demand of the moral reason that the cosmic process shall be moral.

Such then is the Biblical conception of the meaning of history and of the goal of the historic movement. If we would realise how great and satisfying it is, we must contrast it with other conceptions.

Consider first the ancient Pagan conception. "The philosophy", says Martineau, "as well as the poetry of "Greece and Rome had its dream of a golden age when "gods and men dwelt undistinguished, with no desires "but those of innocence, no love but that of justice, no "appetites that transgressed the simplicity of nature. "The guilty passions which had interrupted this flow "of peace had acquired an ascendency more and more "terrible, till nothing was to be expected from an "enraged and disappointed Providence than that some "deluge should sweep away the polluted race, and "prepare a cleansed earth for a new creation of "humanity. Had this been the whole of the Pagan "theory there would have been in it nothing character-"istic,—nothing to distinguish it strikingly from the "Hebrew theology. But the genius of the Heathen "system, its alliance, not with any high moral senti-"ment, but with the cycles of the material universe,— "appears in this; that after its great catastrophe of "destructive flood, all things were again to return in the "same order; the same individual men to be born again, "to act again in the same scenes, and produce the same "series of events; and conduct the world once more "through the same melancholy succession of corruptions "back into chaos and destruction. The whole theory of "society, expounded by the wisest Pagan philosophy of "the Stoical School, is comprised in the weary idea of

"incessant revolution,—of rotation without progress,—
"rotation as of an eccentric wheel, fast sinking and slow
"rising;—an idea incapable of any grandeur except
"that which it may borrow from immense duration,
"and the solemn periodicity of Fate" (*National Duties*,
pp. 296, 7 compressed).

Or, take the view of modern materialism. According
to this view the human race is destined to complete
extinction, when the earth shall no longer be able to
sustain life. Our history will have been but a noisy
moment in the Eternal Silence, destined to be swallowed
up in the oblivion of the Infinite Past.

The ancient theory deprives history of all rational
purpose and end; the modern theory gives it an end
that is the negation of rationality. The Biblical conception alone makes history rational alike in its course
and in its end.

But is the Biblical conception true? Is history
indeed tending towards this goal? It is, at least in
part, simply a question of observation and experience.
Well; I think that history *is* tending towards this goal.
As we study the centuries that lie between us and the
prophets of Israel, we can, I think, discern that the *trend*
of human things has been towards a universal brotherhood and a world-wide faith. And in our own age the
most characteristic movements are the social and the
missionary movements. Doubtless the movement has
been painfully slow; there have been many periods of
wandering, of stagnation, of retrogression; and the end
is still afar off. But as the astronomer who knows a
part of the orbit of a planet can predict its future position, so we may, perhaps, know enough of the curve and
sweep of history to feel justified in believing that it is

moving towards the final unity of mankind in God[1]. We, perhaps, can see this now. But how strong and penetrating must have been the insight of the men who first saw it,—saw it in a world of polytheisms, exclusive nationalities, and robber empires; and saw, moreover, what has most certainly come to pass, that the mightiest impulse of the movement would proceed from their own small and insignificant race! The transcendental consummation of the historic movement in the Unseen and Eternal Order cannot, from the nature of the case, be a matter of present observation and experience. But, as we have seen, it is a postulate of the moral reason, needed to justify our belief in the intrinsic worth of human personality and in the rationality of the universe. We may apply to it the words:—

> "Is it a dream?
> Nay, but the lack of it the dream,
> And failing it, life's love and wealth a dream,
> And all the world a dream".

[1] This drift of history towards unification of the race has been traced by J. H. Crawford, *Brotherhood of Mankind.*

CHAPTER X

BIBLICAL INTERPRETATION OF THE SELF-MANI-
FESTATION OF GOD IN HISTORY (CONTINUED)

WE have seen that the Biblical writers with unparalleled clearness discerned God present and operative
in history ; that He was working out a purpose therein;
and that that purpose was the establishment of a kingdom of the good.   But God effects His purposes by the
use of means, so uniformly applied that we speak of
them as "laws".   At least so it is in nature, and we
expect to find it so in history.   Yet, as we have already
remarked, history seems to the mass of men but a vast
chaos and tangle of events wholly devoid of law and
order.   It was the further glory of the historians and
prophets of Israel that they discerned certain great lines
of law running through this chaos,—certain uniform
methods by which history's great design was being
wrought out.   We have now to see what these methods
are.

I.   The first great method discerned by the Biblical
writers is the method of Election.   One of the most
outstanding features of human life and history is the
vast inequality of endowment and opportunity that may

be observed. All through history we find side by side the man or nation with rich endowment and opportunity and the man or nation with poor endowment and opportunity. This fact is to ordinary view one of the most disturbing features in the Divine government of the world. Religious minds have tried to acquiesce in it as the "inscrutable decree" of the Almighty, Who can do what He will with His own, and to Whom no creature may dare to say, Why hast Thou made me thus? This is the position of Calvinism[1]. Men of an irreligious bent have maintained that the inequalities in question prove the Divine government to be radically unjust. Yet other minds, abandoning the theological point of view, see in these inequalities simply the outcome of the brute struggle for existence. Quite other is the Biblical interpretation. It is that the man or nation of high endowment is endowed not solely for his or its own sake, but also for special service to mankind, considered as the subject of the Kingdom of God, and that endowments and opportunities are bestowed with this universal end in view. They are not private property but a public trust. Should the holder, man or nation, boastfully claim them as signs of Divine favouritism, and use them as the means of self-aggrandisement to the neglect of the wider interest, the privileges are forfeited, and that man or nation is rejected. Such is the Biblical doctrine of

---

[1] It might seem to be also St Paul's position in Rom. ix. But we must not isolate that chapter from the context. It is only one stage in a discussion which is carried on through the two succeeding chapters. The conclusion reached by the Apostle (ch. xi. 32 ff.), viz., that "Election" and "Rejection" are but means in the evolution of a world-wide purpose of mercy, is very different from the Calvinistic conclusion. The word "election" has been so spoiled by the Calvinistic Controversy that it might be well to substitute the word "selection", which bears the same meaning.

Election, which may be defined as the selection and
equipment of a particular man or nation for special
service to mankind considered as the subject of the
Kingdom of God. As was natural, the Hebrew writers
have traced the working of this principle chiefly in their
own national history. It is the philosophy of history
that underlies the very first book of the Bible. "The
purpose of the Book of Genesis," says Professor Sayce,
"is to exemplify the fact of Divine selection". Starting
from undifferentiated humanity, Genesis passes to the
rise of the great distinctions of race. Of these races
one, the Shemitic, is chosen; in this race, one family;
in this family, one man, Abraham; among the children
of Abraham, Isaac; of Isaac's sons, Jacob—the immediate progenitor of Israel. Throughout this process
we are made to see the Divine "purpose working
according to the principle of Selection", rejecting one
man or people, choosing another. And it is to be noted
that "the progress of selection is accompanied by a
corresponding progress in God's revelation of Himself to
the selected few". The aim of the whole process is
declared to be that in the chosen people all the families
of the earth may be blessed[1]. Israel, then, the elect

[1] I am aware that many scholars
maintain that Gen. xii. 3, xviii. 18,
xxii. 18, xxvi. 4, xxviii. 14, are more
correctly rendered "shall bless themselves by thee (or by thy seed)",
i.e., shall desire for themselves the
blessings enjoyed by thee and by thy
seed. The fact is that in the above
passages two different forms of the
Hebrew verb "to bless" are used.
One of these certainly means "to
wish blessing for oneself"; the other
may mean this, but may also mean
"to be blessed". Perhaps it is best
with Professor Driver (hesitatingly

however) to see in the difference of
form a difference of meaning:—
"Three times, it is said, through
"the patriarchs (or their seed) shall
"the families of the earth be blessed;
"twice, in passages perhaps due to
"another hand, it is said that they
"will bless themselves by it, i.e.
"will own it as a source of good,
"and desire for themselves the
"blessings proceeding from it.
"Objectively, in other words, the
"truth of which Israel is the organ
"and channel is to become a
"blessing to the world; and sub-

people *par excellence*, was chosen not solely for its own sake, but for the sake of the world, that it might be the channel of the world-wide diffusion of the knowledge of the living and true God, as saith the Second Isaiah: "I will give thee (Israel) for a light to the nations that thou mayest be my salvation to the ends of the earth". That the prophets of Israel rightly discerned the meaning of their own national history is undoubted: "Ethical "monotheism has been taught the world through the "Jewish race and through it alone". Is there any other instance of a people's teachers attaining so clear a conception of the part their nation was to play in the world? It is easy enough now for us to apply the idea of national vocation, but with them the idea was original : they were the first to give this interpretation to national life. And our wonder increases when we remember that this great idea, if it was not then first conceived, at least received its clearest and grandest expression, at a time when the nation's fortunes were at their lowest ebb: it is one of the "colossally great ideas" of the unknown Prophet of the Exile whom we call the Second Isaiah.

But though the Hebrew writers are naturally concerned with the principle of Election chiefly as it is exemplified in their own national history, they are aware that other men and other nations have their God-given places and tasks in the evolution of the kingdom of God. Amos seeks to abate Israelitish pride by reminding them that, if God had brought them out of Egypt, He had

---

"jectively, it is to be recognised "by the world as such" (*Sermons on the Old Testament*, p. 54; *Commentary on Genesis*, p. 145). But whatever ambiguity may attach to the Genesis passages, other Old Testament passages, notably in Is. xl.—lxvi., unmistakably declare that the nations of the earth shall not only wish for themselves Israel's spiritual blessings, but shall share them.

also brought the Philistines from Caphtor and the Syrians from Kir. And the Second Isaiah speaks of Cyrus as one anointed and called of God to do signal service to the Kingdom, and sees in his career of conquest the fulfilment of the Divine purpose.

That the principle of Election is operative in history is now generally admitted. Some at least of the nations have had a world-wide significance and have fulfilled tasks of world-wide beneficence. We are wont to say that, as to Israel the world owes ethical religion, so to Greece it owes philosophy and art ; to Rome, the science of law ; and, perhaps, to the Anglo-Saxon, the conception of a social life of ordered freedom.

Whether all nations are to be regarded as elect nations, with specific tasks of universal significance, or whether the title belongs properly to a few—the *élite*, as it were, among the peoples—is a question regarding which decision is difficult. China, notwithstanding its vastness and antiquity, seems to have done little for the world. But perhaps the day of China, as of other peoples, is yet to come. In this matter of Election there is what St Paul speaks of as "the fulness of the time". The case of savage peoples that have died out, or are manifestly dying out, is more difficult. They seem to us to have conferred no benefit upon the world in the past, and they have no future. I do not think that we are in a position to pronounce confident judgement until we have decided the question whether their savagery is a primitive condition out of which they have never emerged, or a debased condition into which they have slowly sunk. Race degeneration is a possible thing. Our knowledge of history embraces but an infinitesimal part of man's total life in the world; and it may be that

in some at least of the savage peoples we have but the
relics of races to whom, in pre-historic time, careers of
great beneficence were open, which perhaps they honour-
ably fulfilled,—or faithlessly abandoned. But, be this as
it may, Election is an undoubted law of human life, and
it is a law of the greatest moral value. For men and
nations great endowment and opportunity carry with
them the obligation of service to humanity. The elect
man or nation is but a steward; and sooner or later a
most dread Voice that cannot be denied shall be heard
saying, "Give an account of thy stewardship".

Since Election has always thus a universal end in
view, it follows that the non-elect, if such there be, are,
equally with the elect, the objects of God's gracious
regard: it is for their sakes that the elect are chosen.
Thus, the universal aim involved in Israel's election
shows that the rejection of other nations by God was
apparent only. If it was the Divine intention that
through Israel all the families of the earth should be
blessed, then all the families of the earth must all along
have been the objects of God's beneficent regard. The
temporary religious particularism was but the method by
which a religious universalism was being achieved. And
so it is in all other cases. This being its meaning,
Election entirely loses the appearance of injustice which
it has been so often thought to bear. True, we cannot
tell why this man or this nation has been chosen for a
particular service rather than that man or nation. To
this extent the procedure is, to human view, arbitrary;
but since the end contemplated is the good of all, the
procedure is not unjust. But merely to say of any
Divine procedure that it is not unjust, does not satisfy
a devout mind. The devout mind longs that the world

shall confess that the Divine procedures are positively wise and good. Can this be said of the method of Election? The alternative to the method of Election was a monotonous sameness in excellence and aptitude throughout the human race, all men and all nations, everywhere and always, having the same endowments and aptitudes, and in the same degree, none excelling another in any direction. Now the question is whether under such a system, human nature being what it is, the great human excellences and interests represented by art, science, law, ethics, philosophy, religion, would have been as well conserved and promoted as by the method of Election. So free a thinker as Matthew Arnold thought they would not. Under such a system each of these excellences and interests would have had to take its chance for attention among a multitude of competing interests; with the result that it would have remained, or would have become, feeble and vague. Under the method of Election, while of course these excellences and interests have their roots in general humanity, each of them has been committed as a special trust to some man or nation endowed with special aptitude,—to Israel, ethical religion; to Greece, philosophy and art; to Rome, law, etc. To conserve, develop and promote that interest becomes that people's chief business in life; so, it is not lost in the multiplicity of interests: it is conserved; it receives supreme expression; it is as a city set upon a hill which cannot be hid. And this supreme expression of it becomes an inspiring example to all the world[1]. Election, in fact, is specialization on a cosmic scale; and we ourselves have found that specialization best subserves the great human interests. But there is

---

[1] See M. Arnold, *Literature and Dogma*, p. 41.

more than this to be said. The method of Election directly serves the great end towards which history, under the guidance of God, is tending. That end, as we have seen, is essentially social,—the bringing of all mankind into a Divine-human fellowship. Now the specializing method of Election directly promotes this unifying process; for it necessitates mutual dependence: men and nations have need of one another for the fulness of their life. What living fellowship could there be among units, each of which was perfectly self-contained and fully equipped with all the essentials of life?

The method of Election explains why mankind, originally one, has been differentiated into races and nations, with their physical and mental peculiarities. Such differentiation was necessary for specialization of function. National distinctions thus become an integral part of the Divine Order; and we see why it is that all imperialisms, whether political or ecclesiastical, that have sought to unify mankind by weakening or obliterating national characteristics, have invariably failed. The unity of mankind will come; but not by the method of anti-national imperialism, imposing unity by the forcible suppression of difference, but by the growth of a brotherly spirit among free and mutually serviceable peoples.

In the principle of Election we find, too, the true ground of a nation's obligation to defend its life. National defence should not spring from a blind instinct of self-preservation, but from the conviction that the nation has been called of God to do a service, which it alone can do, to the world. And the same conviction will curb the spirit of wanton aggression upon the life of any other nation. Other nations, too, have their God-given functions, and the weakening or destruction of any of them can only delay the progress of the race towards its goal.

Such then is the first law of the Divine working that the Biblical writers have disclosed to us. Its truth is shown by the light it throws upon otherwise perplexing historical phenomena.

II. The second method of Divine operation discerned by the Biblical writers is that which we now term "Solidarity",—the interdependence for good and evil of man upon man in a community of race, a race being not a congeries of isolated atoms, but a veritable organism. Solidarity is a principle which plays a great part in the sociological thought of our time; but we learnt it from the Old Testament, or, at least, it finds unsurpassed expression there. In the Old Testament Solidarity is seen as a force operating not merely among contemporary men and nations, but also as linking the present to the past, and both to the future. Doubtless all early peoples have a much stronger sense of family, tribal and national unity than have we moderns, in whom the sense of individuality is so much more strongly developed. But I think it is true to say that the feeling of Solidarity was especially strong among the early Hebrews, and that the Biblical writers discerned, as others did not, the function it fulfils in the Divine governance of the world. This sense of Solidarity is seen in their singularly bold and frequent use of personification. For the Biblical writers Egypt, Israel, Babylon, etc., are moral personalities. So vivid and realistic is the personification, that we are apt to think that individual men and women are meant. It is one of the boons of modern Criticism that it enables us to see the large place that personification holds in the

Old Testament.   Thus, in the tenth chapter of Genesis many of us, I doubt not, have thought we were reading the genealogies of individuals.   But this is not so; the chapter is really treating throughout of peoples: the names, though they seem to be personal names, represent, in reality, tribes and sub-tribes[1].   So too, in Gen. xlix. it is the fortunes of tribes, not of individuals, that the dying Jacob forecasts.   So prevalent is personification in Genesis that, as we have seen (ch. VIII.), some scholars deny the presence of any really personal element in the patriarchal narratives, holding that the story throughout represents tribal movements and tribal relations.   We have, however, seen reason for regarding this view as an exaggeration[2].

But personification is not confined to Genesis.   It plays an unsuspectedly large part in the Psalter.   We have all thought, I doubt not, when reading the Psalms that we were reading the strictly personal experiences of individual men.   As a matter of fact, in probably a majority of the Psalms, such is not the case; some modern scholars would say that it is not so in any instance,—that the "I" and the "my" and the "me" of the Psalter is never individual, but always collective— the "I" and the "my" and the "me" of the Church or Nation.   As in Genesis, so here this is probably an exaggeration.   But that in many Psalms which we have been wont to regard as individual, the personified

[1] This is proved by the fact that many of the names are plurals, e.g. Ludim, Anamim, Lehabim, etc.

[2] It is in harmony with this remarkable use of personification that "when it is desired to speak of the "individual members of a tribe or "nation 'sons' ('children') is com- "monly used as in 'children of

"'Israel'".   This example well illustrates how different is our own way of thinking.   We indeed sometimes speak of "Sons of the Empire", but the phrase sounds artificial.   Whereas "child of Israel" was the ordinary way of designating the individual Israelite.

Church or Nation is really the speaker, is beyond question ; and this is so, even when the references seem to be minutely personal.   Take one or two examples :—

> "Much have they afflicted *me* from my *youth* up,
>   Let Israel now say" (Ps. cxxix. 1).

How individual and personal this sounds ; yet the speaker is Israel the Nation.

> "All nations compass *me* about,
>   But in the name of the LORD *I* will destroy them"
>   (cxviii. 10).

Nations do not surround an individual man, nor, if they did, could he destroy them.   The Nation of Israel hard pressed by foes is speaking.   It is as "collectives" that the so-called Imprecatory Psalms are to be understood. These Psalms, as we have seen (ch. VI.), are not the expression of personal resentment against private enemies.   The speaker is the Church or Nation conscious that, for the moment, it represents the cause of God and righteousness, and the objects of the imprecations are the public and insolent enemies of both.

Personification plays a large part also in the Prophets :—

"When Israel was a child, then I loved him and called my son out of Egypt....I taught Ephraim to walk" (Hosea xi. 1, 3).

"Gray hairs are here and there upon him" (*that is*, upon Israel ; Hosea vii. 9).

> "Hearken unto me, O house of Jacob,
>   And all the remnant of the house of Israel,
>   Who are borne by me from the womb,
>   Who are carried from the lap,
>   And even to old age I am the same,
>   And even to gray hairs I will carry you[1]"
>   (Isaiah xlvi. 3, 4).

[1] See Professor McFadyen, *Messages of the Psalms*, pp. 25 ff.

How realistically personal all this is; and yet the subject is the people of Israel. The prophetic writings abound in such personification.

I have said enough to show you how profoundly the Biblical writers realised the principle of Solidarity,— of a net-work of relationships knitting past, present and future generations into one moral organism. And just as clearly did they perceive the function that Solidarity fulfils in the Divine governance of the world. Solidarity is the conserving, diffusing and transmitting principle in human life: it conserves and hands on the accumulated results of the past; and it diffuses over wide areas influences and movements that originate with particular men or peoples. It is thus one great instrument of progress. Without the principle of Solidarity we should all have to begin at the beginning, and we of to-day should be no further forward than primeval man. But, as it is, what each of us inherits from the past, or receives from contemporary men, far exceeds what he achieves by his own efforts. Nevertheless, *a priori* we might count Solidarity a somewhat ambiguous instrument of human well-being and advancement. For must it not conserve, transmit and diffuse evil as well as good? Now undoubtedly this is the case; but not in anything like the same degree. The good that we inherit is larger and more enduring than the evil. The proof is, that, as a matter of fact, the race has progressed. Were it otherwise, we should be experiencing ever accelerating retrogression and deterioration. It is the failure to recognise the Solidarity in good as well as, and more than, in evil that is the real error in the doctrine of Original Sin, at least in its conventional form. That doctrine has rightly called attention to the transmission of evil, which is an undoubted fact of experience, but it has ignored the more abundant transmission of good, which is equally an experienced fact. Now the Biblical writers did not fall into this error. They recognise, and have taught us to recognise, both effects of Solidarity, and in their true proportions. The proof is, that the truth is enunciated in one of the fundamental laws of Hebrew religion and morality, the Second Commandment—" Visiting the iniquity of the fathers upon the "children unto the third and fourth generation of them "that hate me, and showing mercy unto the thousandth "generation ('thousands[1]') of them that love me and "keep my commandments". The transmission of good is the proper function of Solidarity, which hands on the good to a thousand generations, that is, practically for ever. That evil is also transmitted, is an incidental and temporary accompaniment,—only unto the third and fourth generation. We must remember that when once a particular method of governing the universe had been adopted, perhaps not even God, be it reverently spoken, could avoid the disadvantages of that method, or combine with it the advantages that some other method might offer. The very idea of method implies limitation; and the only practical question is, Do the advantages of the particular method followed sufficiently

---

[1] "Thousands" in the Commandment is ambiguous. It may mean the thousands of individuals who are the contemporaries of the obedient man, and to whom he proves a source of blessing. Or, it may mean the thousandth generation of his posterity, to whom he transmits blessing. In either case the principle of Solidarity is affirmed— the influence of good deeds extends far beyond the doer ; but the latter interpretation gives a more exact antithesis to the " third and fourth" generation of the previous clause, and is the interpretation adopted in Deut. vii. 9. The ambiguity is due to the fact that the Hebrew language has no word for "thousandth"; writers were obliged to use the cardinal number.

outweigh the disadvantages to justify the price? That the method of Solidarity stands this practical test experience would seem to show. Notwithstanding the transmission of evil the race progresses; there must therefore be an overplus of good. Once more, then, the Biblical writers throw welcome light upon the perplexing phenomena of history.

III. Another law of the Divine working discerned with especial clearness by the Biblical writers is the law of Retribution. For the Biblical writers, owing to their view of Solidarity, nations are moral personalities, and, as such, subject to the moral law. A commercial age, indeed, is apt to regard a nation as a sort of joint stock company; but, in truth, there is no comparison between the two forms of association. The one is purely a voluntary association formed with a single end in view— the material interests of the promoters. Its rules are rules of expediency, alterable at will, and those who formed it may dissolve it. The other is a natural unity, existing independently of the individual, and is a Divine creation. This is proved by the existence of distinct national types, and by the age-long persistence of these, despite the operation of forces tending to obliterate their differences. Thus, notwithstanding the close association of English, Scotch, Irish, Welsh, in the United Kingdom, these different types show no signs of becoming merged in one uniform type. The true conception of the nation has been nobly expressed by Burke. "The State", he says, "ought not to be considered nothing more than a "partnership agreement in a trade of pepper and coffee, "calico or tobacco, or some other such low concern, to "be taken up for a little temporary interest, and to be "dissolved by the fancy of the parties. It is to be

"looked upon with other reverence, because it is not a
"partnership in things subservient only to the gross
"animal existence of a temporary perishable nature.
"It is a partnership in all science ; a partnership in all
"arts; a partnership in every virtue and in all perfection.
"As the ends of such a partnership cannot be obtained
"in many generations, it becomes a partnership not only
"between those who are living, but between those who
"are dead and those who are to be born. Each contract
"of each particular State is but a clause in the great
"primeval contract of eternal society, linking the lower
"with the higher natures, connecting the visible and the
"invisible world, according to a fixed compact sanctioned
"by the inviolable oath which holds all physical and all
"moral natures each in their appointed place[1]".

It is one of the permanent values of the Old Testament, strangely overlooked in our time, that more fully
than any other book in the world, it sets forth the
Divine foundations upon which this conception, true as
it is noble, of national life alone can rest. No people
ever had such a sense of nationality as the Hebrews,—a
fact proved by their preservation of national distinctness
throughout their age-long and world-wide dispersion.
A nation, then, being such a unity as we have described,
is rightly conceived by the Biblical writers as the subject
of moral law. It is on this principle that the prophets
interpret the most awful problem of history—the downfall of nations. Whatever secondary causes may have
contributed to the result, the prophets are sure that when
a nation perishes it is the righteous Retribution of God

---

[1] Burke *seems* to hold the "contract theory" of the State, but as
Professor Rashdall comments, "A
"contract which was never made
"and which can never be dissolved
"has become a metaphor" (*Christus
in Ecclesia*, pp. 295–6).

The Old Testament may almost be said to be one vast
procession of nations going to their doom—Israel,
Judaea, Assyria, Babylonia.   The spectacle fascinates
the prophets and inspires some of their grandest
utterances[1].   If, at times, they feel an awe-full joy when
some tyrannous empire, "that smote peoples in wrath
with a continual stroke", falls at last, they are not
unmoved by the piteousness of it all, when cities, that
once teemed with full and vigorous life, become silent
and desolate, "and wild beasts of the desert lie there,
"and their houses are full of doleful creatures, and ostriches
"dwell there, and satyrs dance there, and wolves cry in
"their castles, and jackals in the pleasant palaces[2]".

Now it is a fact that nations fall.   The shores of
history are strewn with the wreck of peoples that once
were mighty and played a great part in the world.   How
are we to explain the fact?   We know the explanation
that is fashionable just now.   It is this.   Starting from
the conception that a nation is an organism, analogous
to animal organisms, the analogy is pressed to the point
of finding in nations exactly the same life-history as
that which obtains in the animal kingdom.   As animals

---

[1] Read, e.g., Isaiah's Ode on the downfall of Babylon, ch. xiii.
[2] "There is a silence where hath been no sound;
        There is a silence where no sound may be;
        In the cold grave—under the deep, deep sea,
    Or in wide desert where no life is found,
    Which hath been mute, and still must sleep profound;
        No voice is hushed—no life treads silently,
        But clouds and cloudy shadows wander free,
    That never spoke, over the idle ground.
    But in green ruins, in the desolate walls
        Of antique palaces, where Man hath been,
    Though the dun fox, or wild hyaena, calls,
        And owls, that flit continually between,
    Shriek to the echo, and the low winds moan,
    There the true silence is, self-conscious and alone".

                                        THOMAS HOOD.

pass through the successive stages of infancy, youth, maturity, old age, death, so, it is thought, do nations. In the one case as in the other these stages are natural and inevitable. Decay and death claim animal and nation alike at last. This seems to be the view adopted by Mr Kidd in *Social Evolution*[1]. "We see", he says, "social systems born in silence and obscurity. "They develop beneath our eyes. They make progress "until they exhibit a certain maximum of vitality. "They gradually decline, and finally disappear, having "presented in the various stages certain well-marked "phases which invariably accompany the development "and dissolution of organic life wheresoever encountered. "It may be observed too that this idea of the life, "growth and decline of peoples is deeply rooted. It is "always present in the mind of the historian. It is "to be met with continually in popular literature. The "popular imagination is affected by it. It finds con- "stant expression in the utterances of public speakers "and of writers in the daily press, who, ever and "anon, remind us that our national life, or, it may be, "the life of our civilisation, must reach, if it has not "already reached, its stage of maximum development, "and that it must decline like others which have pre- "ceded it" (*Social Evolution*, p. 98). I cannot but count this view of national destiny to be most pernicious. In young communities it must foster a fatal optimism, as though they had, necessarily and of course, a long and prosperous career before them; in old communities, an equally fatal pessimism. What could be more be- numbing, what could more effectually bring about the catastrophe it foresees, than that a whole people should

[1] See E. A. Eagar, *City of God* (Appendix).

become possessed of the conviction that its inevitable decline had set in? Upon what then is the theory based? It is based (1) upon the observed fact that in the past nations generally have declined and fallen, thus suggesting the operation of some general law. (2) Upon the identification of this law with the biological law of successive stages of growth and decay, which we see to be universally operative in animal organisms. But is there not here some confusion of thought? Is it simply because it is an organism that an animal grows old and dies, or, is it rather because it is an organism composed of constituents of a certain kind? Surely this latter. The conception of an organism does not in itself involve the idea of successive stages ending in dissolution; one has no difficulty in conceiving an organism that should grow and live for ever. It is the nature of the constituents of the animal organism that determines its peculiar life-history. The mere fact then that a nation is an organism does not of itself involve a similar life-history, if the constituents are not similar. Nations do die; but the real and ultimate cause may be quite other than biological. The prophets and historians of the Bible assert that the cause is quite other; that in the doom of nations we are to see the operation, not of biological, but of moral, law,—the retributive action of the Power that makes for righteousness, dealing with nations, as with men, according to their works. This view is as sobering and as stimulating as the biological theory is deluding and paralysing. There is no inevitableness about a nation's fate, whether in its youth or in its maturity. A nation's moral character shapes its destiny; and its moral character rests with itself to make or to mar. How are we to decide between the conflicting theories?

It would seem to be a question of observation and experience. Mr Kidd says that the biological theory is ever in the mind of the historian. He forgets the Biblical writers, who have not so read history. But though they are the supreme exponents of the retributive view, other observers of history, both in ancient and modern times, have maintained that moral retribution is a determining factor in national life. It was a leading idea with the earliest of Greek historians, Herodotus. "To him", says Professor Butcher, "the course of the "world, its incidents great and small, are under Divine "governance. The same 'forethought' or providence "which is at work in maintaining a just balance of forces "within the animal kingdom, likewise presides over the "destinies of empires. This supreme power...humiliates "human pride, it lures on insolence to its ruin, it pursues "the guilty through generations. And as in Jewish "history the fortunes of Israel intermingle with the "secular currents of universal history, so in Herodotus "Greek history is read in its larger and world-wide rela-"tions. The great military monarchies pass before our "eyes in a series of apparent digressions ; but the main "theme is never forgotten ; the tragic action moves "onward through retarding incidents, till at last the "Divine Retribution hastens towards its goal, and all the "pride of the East, gathered into one under Persia, "flings itself in foreordained ruin on the free land of "Hellas[1]".

And the same interpretation of history is given by moderns who have in no way been pledged to an unquestioning acceptance of the Bible. "One lesson", says Froude, "and only one, history may be said to

[1] *Harvard Lectures on Greek subjects*, p. 32.

"repeat with distinctness; that the world is built some-
"how on moral foundations; that in the long run it is
"well with the good; in the long run it is ill with the
"wicked". And again, "It (history) is a voice for ever
"sounding across the centuries the laws of right and
"wrong. For every false word or unrighteous deed, for
"cruelty and oppression, for lust or vanity, the price has
"to be paid at last; not always by the chief offenders,
"but by some one. Justice and truth alone endure and
"live. Injustice and falsehood may be long-lived, but
"doomsday comes at last to them, in French revolutions
"and other terrible ways" (*Short Studies*, pp. 21, 27).
Matthew Arnold, in *Literature and Dogma*, with emphatic
approval thus sums up the Biblical doctrine : " Down they
"come, one after another; Assyria falls, Babylon, Greece,
" Rome ; they all fall for want of *conduct*, righteousness....
"Judaea itself, the holy land, the land of God's Israel,
"falls too, and falls for want of righteousness". It is
this view of history that I suppose Lord Acton, the
profoundest student of history in our time, had in mind
when he wrote, "There is no escape from the dogma
that history is the conscience of mankind". But it is
to be observed that it is not only the internal life of
nations, as expressed in the mutual relations of their
citizens, that is thus subject to the action of moral law.
The Biblical writers (e.g. Amos) perceived that moral
law governs the external life as well,—their international
relations. Indeed, when we speak of a nation as forming
a separate organism and living a distinct life, we are
contrasting it not so much with its own citizens (though
that contrast exists) as with other national unities. Now
the Biblical doctrine is that the mutual relations of nations
are as truly amenable to moral law as the mutual re-

lations of persons; "that between State and State, as
"between person and person, the right and true has
"eternal obligation". It cannot be said that this truth
has ever received adequate recognition in international
politics. Many people, perhaps most, would deny that
it is a truth at all ; they would quite confidently assert
that in their mutual dealings nations can know no law
but that of self-interest. Yet it is possible that in this
matter popular opinion may be miserably wrong, and
that a deeper reading of history would teach that the
mutual relations of nations, not less than of persons,
come within the sweep of an inexorable Justice. The
doctrine of Retribution, then, is the third great line of
law, discerned by the Biblical writers, as running through
the tangle of history. If we can receive it, it will save
us from the pessimism which the downfall of mighty
nations might otherwise beget in us. Regard that
downfall as a Fate or a Caprice and you will hardly
escape pessimism. But pessimism can have no place
when it is seen that the destiny of nations is determined
by eternal Righteousness.

IV. Another great principle discerned by the Biblical
writers as operative in history is that of the fruitfulness
of Vicarious Suffering. Perhaps no problem of human
life and history so occupied the minds of the sages of
Israel as the problem of suffering. One whole book
of the Old Testament, in some respects the greatest of
them all, the Book of Job, is entirely concerned with
this problem. The reason is to be found in Israel's pure
and lofty conception of God. To the man or nation
who believes in cruel and capricious deities, or in no
deities at all, suffering, properly speaking, presents no
problem ; it may lacerate the heart, but cannot offend

the conscience.   It is otherwise with all who believe in
a merciful and righteous God : for these the problem
of suffering is urgent.   The first solution found by
Israel was that suffering is penal ; and there can be no
doubt that much of the suffering of the world—far more
than we like to think—is the direct outcome of sin.   And
so far as it is so, it of course presents no problem to the
conscience ; for we ourselves inflict suffering upon wrong-
doers, and think it right to do so.   But in course of
time it was perceived that the retributive solution was
too narrow; that not wrong-doers alone suffered, but also
the innocent, and, more perplexing still, the positively
righteous.   This is the real problem, that in a world
governed by a righteous God the innocent and the
righteous suffer, and are sometimes the greatest sufferers.
Now, passing by the suffering that arises from the action
of the natural elements, such as that caused by tempest,
volcano, earthquake, which, though impressive to the
imagination, is really infinitesimal in amount[1], the undeserved suffering in the world is wholly, or almost
wholly due to the principle of Solidarity, which we have
already considered.   And it is due to Solidarity in two
respects : to Solidarity as a fact; and to Solidarity's
function in the world.   The innocent suffer through the
fact of Solidarity ; the righteous suffer through the *function* of Solidarity.   Let us consider both these aspects
of the case.   Solidarity means, as we have seen, that
we are all bound together by a net-work of relationships,
whereby it results that, to an indefinite extent, we are
all at one another's mercy.   The consequences of our

---

[1] For a luminous treatment of the
suffering arising from the physical
elements see Martineau, *Introduction*
to the Study of Religion, vol. II.
pp. 83 ff. (2nd ed.).

actions, good or bad, extend far beyond ourselves, and
involve the happiness of other people. Thus, a selfish or
careless householder, by neglecting the drainage of his
house, may infect a whole neighbourhood ; a profligate
father involves his family in disease or poverty or shame ;
a reckless, incompetent or corrupt statesman brings
disaster upon his country. In all these cases the sufferers
are innocent, in the sense that, whatever their personal
faults, they are not guilty of the acts that have caused
the suffering. They are the victims of the wrong-doings
of others, over whom perhaps they have had no control.
Now it is the fact of Solidarity that makes this possible.
But it is not the innocent only who suffer through Solidarity ; the righteous not seldom suffer through it. But
there is this difference: the innocent suffer *in spite of*
their innocence; whereas the righteous suffer *because of*
their righteousness. This latter results from Solidarity's
function. As we have seen, Solidarity is the con-
servative element in human nature : it conserves what
has already been attained. It thus ministers to progress ;
but it is not itself a directly progressive principle ; it is
rather static than dynamic and propulsive. Its chief
effect indeed is to produce and maintain a respectable
average. The progressive element in human history is
not man in the mass, but man the individual. Progress
springs from great personalities who see further, and feel
more deeply, than their fellows (see ch. v.). A man
arises to whom has come the vision of a higher and
more heroic type of life than the time affects, or who
perceives some duty that his generation is neglecting,
or some monstrous evil that it is tolerating. He feels
that he must go forth to disclose the vision, to exhort
to the neglected duty, to denounce the tolerated evil.

And he is met by the stolid inertia of Solidarity's average, and all its allies—Reverence for the past, Dread of innovation, Fear of disturbing what has worked well enough, Indifference, Prejudice, Vested Interests.   Here then are all the elements of a conflict.   The weapons on the one side are truth and conviction ; on the other, in robust ages, the hemlock cup, the gibbet, the dungeon, the stake ; in a feebler age, vituperation, calumny, scorn, contempt, ostracism.   And you have one of the darkest problems of history—a Sufferer for Righteousness' sake.

Such then are the two ways in which Solidarity may operate to cause undeserved suffering.   Now what is to be said ?   Well, we have seen that the evils that arise from Solidarity are of the nature of incidental accompaniments.   Solidarity's proper function is not to cause evil, but to conserve good ; and indeed the stubbornness of its resistance to new forms of good is the measure of the tenacity with which it retains them, when once it has admitted them.   If then it can be shown that upon the whole it effects more good than ill, we may perhaps be content.   We do not know that any other method of governing the moral universe would produce better results, or that any other method is even possible.   But it must be allowed that the argument from ignorance rather silences than satisfies.   However, the prophets of Israel were not content to leave the problem of undeserved suffering a wholly unsolved mystery.   They sought and found a solution ; and it is this : that in the Divine governance of the world, Vicarious Suffering becomes a fruitful seed, from which a more abundant harvest of good is eventually reaped.   This fruitfulness of Vicarious Suffering is perhaps the most beautiful law of the moral universe ; for it shows that even the incidental evils of Solidarity are made to subserve the main design. True it is chiefly in the undeserved suffering of the righteous that the Biblical writers trace the operation of this law; but the clue once placed in our hands, we can for ourselves trace its operation in all Vicarious Suffering.

The passages in which the law is most fully stated are Ps. xxii. and Is. lii. 13—liii. 12. In both passages we have a Sufferer. Since the days of the Ethiopian eunuch, men have been asking, Of whom do Psalmist and Prophet speak? Of themselves or of some other? With diffidence I suggest that *consciously* they speak neither of themselves nor of any other concrete person; but that in both passages we have suffering for righteousness' sake personified and idealised. Neither Psalmist nor Prophet nor any contemporary of theirs suffered just all that is here described, nor did any sufferings endured in that age produce the consequences that are here described[1]. It is indeed very probable that some of the details in both portraitures have been drawn from the writers' own experience, or from the experience of past or contemporary sufferers for righteousness' sake; but the completed portraitures are ideal. The writers have conceived a perfectly righteous Sufferer, whose sufferings are inflicted upon him by his fellow men solely because of his righteousness, and they tell us that such sufferings, patiently borne, so far from proving the defeat of righteousness, assure its greatest triumph; with the implication that all undeserved suffering, in proportion as it approximates to the ideal, will have a like result.

[1] I believe of course that both Psalm and Prophecy were realised in Jesus Christ. But in the text I am considering what the writers had consciously in mind.

In the Psalm the Sufferer is represented as himself
discovering the beautiful meaning of his suffering ; in the
prophecy nations and kings are represented as looking
back upon the suffering as a thing of the past, and
declaring that experience has shown its fruitfulness.
Accordingly, in the Psalm the Sufferer is the speaker.
He is perplexed by his sufferings. He turns to God
and plaintively asks why He thus abandons His servant
to the will of the wicked. He describes his sufferings,
which include every form of misery and wrong that
malice can devise. He betrays no resentment ; he impre-
cates no vengeance ; he simply pours forth his plaint to
the Ever Holy. Suddenly there flashes upon him the
meaning of it all: it will achieve the world-wide triumph
of the Kingdom of God for which he suffers ; he is filled
with hope and is glad :—

> " All the ends of the earth shall remember and return unto
>   JEHOVAH,
>   And all the families of the nations shall bow down before Thee.
>   For the kingdom is JEHOVAH'S,
>   And He is ruler among the nations ".

In the Isaian passage we are transported into the
future. The Sufferer and his suffering belong to the
past. Nations and kings, looking back with wonder
and awe, reverently tell the story : how he was despised
and rejected of men ; how they had counted him as a
wrong-doer smitten by the just judgement of God ; his
silent endurance ; how none of his contemporaries guessed
the true meaning of his woes. But time has disclosed
the secret ; they see it all now ; they confess with shame
the injustice that had been done, and gratefully acknowledge that the suffering of the Righteous One has brought
them peace and healing and righteousness.

That the fruitfulness of the Vicarious Suffering of the righteous, enunciated by psalmist and prophet, is a fact of the moral universe, is now universally admitted. "The great agent", says Renan, "of the march of the "world is pain...There are always voluntary agents "ready to serve the ends of the universe". "O joy "supreme of the virtuous man. The world hangs on "him. He is one in a thousand thousands, but it is he "who is the ransom of Sodom". "It (Vicarious Suffering) is", says President Hyde, "a universal law of which "the cross of Christ is the eternal symbol. It is the "price someone must pay for every step of progress and "every conquest over evil the world shall ever gain[1]". And the great world of common men agree that it is. Whom does the world consent to retain in its memory? Not the men who amassed great fortunes, who while they lived did well unto themselves. Of these the memory perishes. But the sufferers for righteousness' sake. These the world believes to be its greatest bene-factors, and it holds them in everlasting remembrance.

The *rationale* of the fruitfulness of suffering for right-eousness' sake is perhaps not difficult, at least in part, to discern. It is, I think, largely due to moral impression and reaction. Man is made in the image of God. That fundamental part of his moral constitution he never wholly loses. It follows that at bottom there is an affinity between the spirit of man and the truth and righteousness of God. Human nature, as we know it, is indeed alien from the Divine Kingdom; of this we need no further proof than is afforded by the huge amount of undeserved suffering of which human nature

---

[1] Quoted by A. B. Bruce in *Providential Order*,—a book which has suggested to me the line of thought followed in this chapter.

has been the cause. Nevertheless the alienation does not penetrate to the bottom. Conscience remains, living if asleep. And among the appeals that may arouse it, none is more powerful than suffering patiently endured for righteousness' sake. Robed in a vesture of suffering, Righteousness appears before men's eyes "apparelled in celestial light"; it is felt to be real; it acquires a new value when it is seen to win such disinterested service; over against it evil is seen in its true colours. Indignation, reverence, admiration are evoked; a moral revulsion sets in; and men look on those whom they have pierced and mourn because of them. As the result a new ideal is given to the world, and ever after

> "   —the memory of noble deeds
> Cries shame upon the idle and the vile,
> And keeps the heart of man for ever up
> To the heroic level of old time[1]".

The Biblical writers have not so emphatically affirmed the fruitfulness of the Vicarious Suffering of the innocent[2]; but the same law holds good. The suffering of the innocent is also, in its degree, a fruitful thing, and by the same process of moral impression and reaction. That the consequences of sin are not confined to the sinner but extend to the innocent and the dear, even to the third and fourth generation, is fitted to make, and does make, a profound impression upon the conscience. It makes men—some men at least—shrink from sin, even when sin is most alluring. It subdues to penitence hearts that have resisted all other appeals. In the in-

---

[1] Lowell, *Prometheus*.

[2] The question of the suffering of the innocent is dealt with by Ezekiel (ch. xviii.), but only as it affects the sufferer, that being the aspect of the case with which those whom he immediately addresses were occupied.

nocent sufferers themselves it implants a salutary hatred of the sin that has so deeply wounded them, and a stern resolve that they in their turn will not be guilty of so foul a wrong. To the world at large it is a standing memento of the exceeding evil of sin.

Such then is the Biblical conception of Vicarious Suffering. That it is a true interpretation we all probably admit: Vicarious Suffering *is* fruitful.

But perhaps we have not observed what I have been trying to point out, the beautiful way in which the evil, incidental to the principle of Solidarity, is counteracted, and more than counteracted, by being itself made an instrument of more abundant good. But it may be said, Granted that, on the whole and in the long run, the world at large is being benefited by Vicarious Suffering, is it not at the cost of a huge injustice to the sufferers; and how can this be reconciled with the righteousness of God? I cannot but think that this objection derives much of its force from our failing fully to distinguish between Vicarious Suffering and vicarious punishment. The distinction is this: the victim of Vicarious Suffering suffers *through* the fault of another; the victim of vicarious punishment suffers *for* the fault of another. The distinction is not merely verbal; but is one which in human affairs the conscience fully recognises, as an illustration will show. A general, let us say, sends a soldier to take at the cost of his life, a post which was lost by the carelessness of someone else. That soldier *suffers* vicariously. The same general knowingly hangs a soldier for an offence committed by someone else. That soldier is *punished* vicariously[1]. Now does the

---

[1] I owe this illustration to Professor Jellett.

conscience pronounce the same judgement upon these two cases of undeserved suffering? By no means. In the latter case it affirms that the general has committed a frightful crime; in the former case it affirms that he has done his bounden duty. I suppose the ground of the distinction is in part this: in the former case an end is gained which ought to be dear to the sufferer himself, viz., the safety or victory of his country; in the latter case no end is gained: rather the end of all punishment —the vindication of justice—is frustrated. Be this as it may, conscience approves the one as unhesitatingly as it condemns the other. Now to which of the two cases is the undeserved suffering of the world allied? Plainly to the former,—to Vicarious Suffering, not to vicarious punishment. Now, the suffering of the soldier sent to retake the lost position, is really an instance of the principle of Solidarity; and we have seen that to Solidarity is due the undeserved suffering of the world. But conscience cannot reasonably object to an element in the moral government of the world which, in an analogous sphere, it entirely approves. But there is something more to be said. I have said that the end for which the soldier suffers vicariously ought to be dear to him; yet of course it may not; his may be no willing sacrifice. But the end for which the sufferer for righteousness' sake suffers, *is* dear to him; he is a willing victim, else he were not righteous. And for all undeserved suffering, whether of the innocent or the righteous, it is the Biblical teaching that there are abundant compensations in that perfect future where they that sow in tears shall reap in joy.

V. There is one more method of the Divine ordering of history to which I must draw your attention, viz., the

doctrine of the Remnant. " The idea of the Remnant ",
says Professor Sanday, " is one of the most typical
" and significant in the prophetic portions of the Old
" Testament ". It is the conviction that apostasy and
corruption can never go the length of the entire extinction of goodness or the complete frustration of the
gracious purpose of God for the race ; that there is
always hidden away, even in the darkest times, a Faithful
Remnant—a seed of better hope—affording some firm
ground for the assurance that righteousness must ultimately triumph in a world that, for the moment, may
seem wholly to lie in wickedness. This idea appears
first in the history of Elijah, who, when he complains
that he is left alone in his jealousy for the LORD of
Hosts, is assured by the " still small voice " that, in the
sifting judgement which is about to overtake a degene-
rate age, there will be found left seven thousand—" all
"the knees that have not bowed to Baal, and every mouth
"which hath not kissed him ". Henceforth this idea of an
imperishable seed of righteousness becomes one of the
root convictions of all Israel's prophets. But Isaiah is
its great exponent. So strongly is he possessed by it
that he embodies it in the very name of one of his sons,
Shear Jashub ("a remnant shall return "). It was this
faith that saved the prophets of Israel, notwithstanding
their strong ethical sense of contemporary evil, from
yielding to pessimism. For pessimism, we must remember, is not the sorrowful recognition of existing
evil and impending judgement,—which may simply be
the recognition of facts. Pessimism is the feeling that
the evil recognised is too wide-spread, too inveterate,
ever to be remedied ; that righteousness must suffer
permanent defeat. This was not the temper of Israel's

prophets; not even of Jeremiah, whose name has been most unjustly used as a synonym for pessimistic lamentation over the ever deepening degeneracy of the world[1]. The prophets were saved from pessimism by their doctrine of the Remnant, of a real though concealed leaven of good in the worst of times.

In his *American Addresses*, Matthew Arnold helps us to realise the power of the Biblical use of the idea of the Remnant by contrasting it with Plato's use of the same idea. With Plato it is a word of despondency. "There is but a very small remnant", he says, "of honest "followers of wisdom, and they who are of these few, "and have tasted how sweet and blessed a possession is "wisdom, and who can see, moreover, the madness of "the multitude, and that there is no one, we may say, "whose action in public matters is sound, and no ally "for whosoever would help the just, what are they to "do? They may be compared to a man who has fallen "among wild beasts; he will not be one of them, but he "is too unaided to make head, and before he can do "any good to society or his friends he will be over "whelmed and perish utterly. When he considers this "he will resolve to keep still, and to mind his own "business; as it were standing aside under a wall in "a storm of dust and hurricane of driving wind; and "he will endure to behold the rest filled with iniquity, "if only he himself may live a life clear of injustice and "impiety, and depart when his time comes, in mild and "gracious mood, with fair hope". The smallness of the remnant of the good is, you see, to Plato—as to classic thought generally (cf. ch. VIII.)—a thought leading, cn

---

[1] Jeremiah has glowing hope of a better future, see e.g., ch. xxxi.

the one hand, to contemptuous despair of the world, and on the other, to a selfish individualism wholly absorbed in saving its own soul. How different is the tone of the Hebrew prophets. " *The Remnant!*—it is the word of "the Hebrew prophets also, and especially it is the word "of the greatest of them all, Isaiah. Not used with the "despondency of Plato, used with far other power in- "forming it, and with a far other future awaiting it, "filled with fire, filled with hope, filled with faith, filled "with joy...¹". In the ardour of their faith in a "holy seed" in the midst of corruption, and in its power to grow and expand and propagate itself, the prophets of Israel may seem to have anticipated a too speedy triumph of righteousness. But that in the principle of the Remnant they discovered a true law of the Divine Government, has been illustrated again and again in human history. Again and again there have been periods of seemingly utter degeneracy when there has seemed to be "no ally for whosoever would help the just", and men have been tempted to save each his own soul, and always there has proved to be a faithful remnant from which a better age has sprung. If we seek the secret of the invincible hope of the Hebrew prophet, as contrasted with the despondency of the Greek thinker, it is to be found not in any sentimental, luxurious optimism which refuses to recognise the reality of evil and the certainty of Divine retribution ; for of both the Hebrew had a profounder sense than the Greek. No ; it is to be found in the prophet's conception of God as the eternally Righteous and Omnipotent. From such a God what triumphs of righteousness may not be expected in the golden future ?

¹ *American Addresses*, pp. 9, 15.

> " Truth, pressed to earth, shall rise again,
> The eternal years of God are hers ".

We have now completed our study of the Old Testament interpretation of history. We may summarise it thus: God, Righteous and All-Sovereign, is the supreme Factor in History. History is not chaotic but purposeful, having as its goal the realisation of the Kingdom of God. This Kingdom is the *summum bonum* for man, as an essentially social and moral personality. Election, Solidarity, Retribution, Vicarious Suffering, the Remnant, are great general methods and laws which control the whole movement.

These principles are writ large in Israel's prophetico-historical literature. They are quite independent of any and every critical theory as to the literary origin and history of the Bible. They are in the Bible in black and white. Whatever else the Bible contains, it contains these principles. And these principles are our only clue amid the mystery and perplexity of human history. Remove them, forget them ; and human history becomes a meaningless phantasmagoria, and we men,

> "   —no better than a moving row
> Of magic shadow-shapes that come and go
> Round with the Sun-illumined Lantern held
> In midnight by the Master of the Show ;
>
> But helpless pieces of the game He plays
> Upon this chequer-board of Nights and Days ;
> Hither and thither moves, and checks and slays,
> And one by one back in the Cupboard lays[1]".

But I believe that observation and experience show them to be true principles,—to be the principles that are

---

[1] Omar Khayyam.

actually governing history; that history is moving, however slowly, towards the unity of mankind in God, and
that the movement is in accordance with such general
laws as the Biblical writers have enunciated.

CONCLUSION.

In the foregoing pages we have seen what is meant
by Biblical Criticism, and also some of the results which
Criticism claims to have reached.   But when Criticism
has done its work, the Old Testament remains. Criticism
has not spirited it away from our book-shelves.   Exam-
ining this Old Testament we have found that, among
other things, it contains an interpretation of the Self-
manifestation of God in Nature, Conscience, and, above
all, in History,—that Self-manifestation in the presence
of which all men perpetually live, and of which they are
dimly conscious when they are conscious of a Something
in Nature, Conscience. History, that is other than themselves and than their fellows.   It is contended in these
pages that this interpretation is shown by observation
and experience to be true ; that it, and it alone, enables
us to feel that we are living in a rational, purposeful and
moral universe ; that it, and it alone, enables us to live
rationally, purposefully and morally ourselves,—which is
for rational and purposeful natures the ultimate criterion
of truth (see pp. 73–75). The question then arises, How
came it about that the Biblical writers, and they alone,
attained to this interpretation in all its fulness ?   It is
contended in these pages that the explanation is, that the
Biblical writers were the subjects of a special operation
of the Spirit of God, which quickened their intellectual,

moral and spiritual faculties, and so enabled them to read aright the open secret of God's Self-manifestation. Inspiration is certainly an adequate explanation. Is there any other equally adequate?

Te prophetarum laudabilis numerus...laudat....

INDEX

www.ingramcontent.com/pod-product-compliance
Ingram Content Group UK Ltd.
Pitfield, Milton Keynes, MK11 3LW, UK
UKHW042143280225
455719UK00001B/58